D1361706

Members' DIY Secrets

Handyman Club of America
Minneapolis, Minnesota

Members' DIY Secrets

Printed in 2004.

Credits

Tom Carpenter
Creative Director

Mark Johanson
Book Products Development Manager

Chris Marshall
Editorial Coordinator

Dan Cary
Photo Production Coordinator

Marti Naughton
Art Director & Production

Steve Anderson
Copy Editor & Production Assistant

Jon Hegge
Photo Production & Photography

Cover Photo

Shop-made cutting guide for hand saws ensures straight, accurate cuts. Photo by Mark Macemon.

ISBN 1-58159-027-X

3 4 5 6 7 8 9 / 09 08 07 06 05 04

Handyman Club of America
12301 Whitewater Drive
Minnetonka, Minnesota 55343
www.handymanclub.com

Foreward

Every time you pick up a magazine or tune in your favorite do-it-yourself TV show, you'll hear someone described as an "expert." At *Handy* magazine, we depend heavily on "experts" with years of professional trades experience to make sure the information we publish is up-to-date and accurate. But over the years we've noticed something interesting here at the Handyman Club of America. More often than not, the most original, creative and useful ideas we see don't come from the experts or the professionals or the highly paid designers and builders. They come from the Members of the Club. And when you stop and think about it, that shouldn't be a surprise. After all, who understands better the challenges most of us face as we pursue our handyman interests: the professional with his hundred-thousand-dollar budget, or the fellow Member whose "clients" are a pair of cherished grandchildren or a down-on-his luck neighbor who needs a helping hand?

In this new book produced by the Handyman Club, you won't find a lot of "expert" advice, but you will find a wealth of ideas, suggestions and projects you can really use. Good ideas, simple solutions to real-life problems, clever tricks for stretching money and tried-and-true secrets that will help you get the most out of your tools, your money and even the discarded scraps that are lying in the corners and drawers of every workshop.

The Handyman Club of America is dedicated to sharing these great ideas and secrets with all our Members. Whether it's in a book or in the Tip Trader or HandyWorks sections of *Handy,* I hope you'll take the time to share your own hard-learned tips and creative project ideas with your fellow Members. Because when it comes to creative thinking and practical solutions, our Members are our greatest resource.

Tom Sweeney

Tom Sweeney
Publisher
Handyman Club of America

IMPORTANT NOTICE

For your safety, caution and good judgement should be used when following instructions described in this book. Take into consideration your level of skill and the safety precautions related to the tools and materials shown. Neither the publisher, North American Membership Group, nor any of their affiliates can assume responsibility for any damage to property or persons as a result of the misuse of the information provided. Consult your local building department for information on permits, codes, regulations and laws that may apply to your project.

Table of Contents

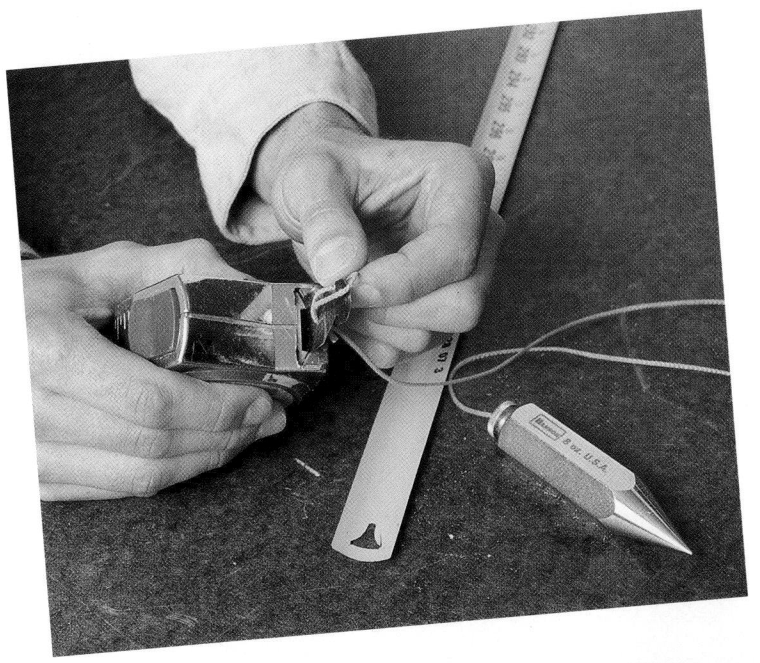

Member Secrets

Member Projects

DELTA
Yellow
Wood
Glue
START
STOP

Member Secrets

Being a handyman is all about solving problems. Whether you're fixing a lamp or building a house, successfully completing the project depends on creative solutions to a series of challenges. In this section of *Members' DIY Secrets*, you'll find page after page of creative solutions to problems encountered by most Club Members. In the workshop, around the house or outdoors, this collection of Members' secrets will make many of your home improvement and workshop tasks easier and help you get better results from your projects.

Handyman Secrets

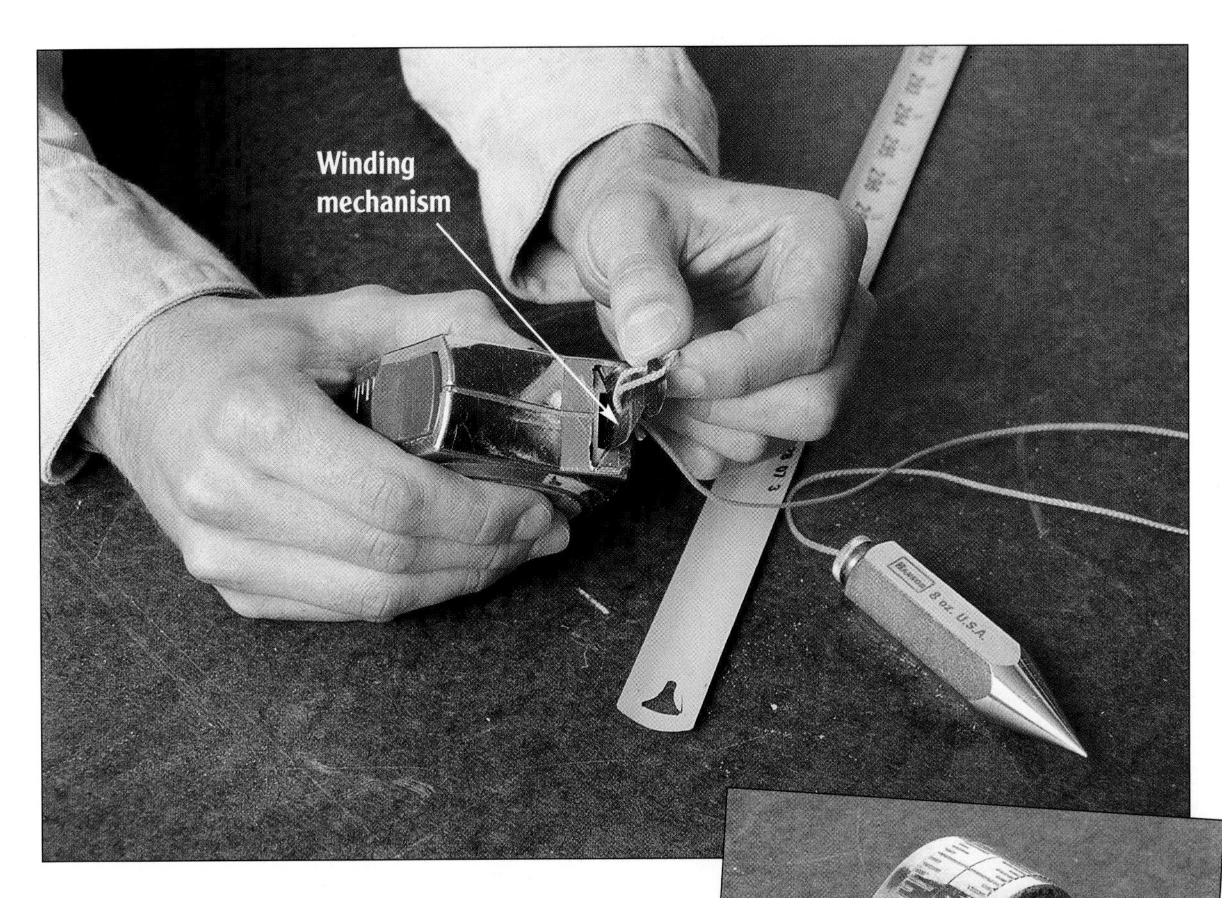

Tape measure transformed to plumb bob

To make myself a handy self-winding plumb bob, I took an old tape measure with a broken tape and pulled out the tape until I reached the end that attaches to the winding mechanism. I detached the tape and replaced it with a length of a 30-ft. mason's line. Then I attached a plumb bob to the other end of the mason's line and let the line wind into the tape measure housing.

With this tool, I don't have to hand-wind the line every time I use my plumb bob. Best of all, the line can never get tangled up with other tools in my toolbox—it's always reeled up and ready to go when I need it.

James Papas
Crockett, California

"Slik" solution unsticks stacked buckets

Everyone who uses five-gallon pails sooner or later ends up struggling to separate two or more buckets stacked inside one another. I'm not sure why the buckets are designed that way, unless some engineer with a twisted sense of humor thought he'd enjoy watching people's veins bulging from their foreheads while trying to separate a stack of buckets!

To put an end to this hassle, I've designed a bucket insert that I call the "slikstik." When two of my simple devices are inserted on either side of each bucket into the slot below the handle, they limit the bucket from sliding too far into the bucket beneath it. The ⅝-in. gap created by the slikstik prevents a vacuum from forming when the two buckets wedge together. With slikstiks installed, buckets slide right out from each other.

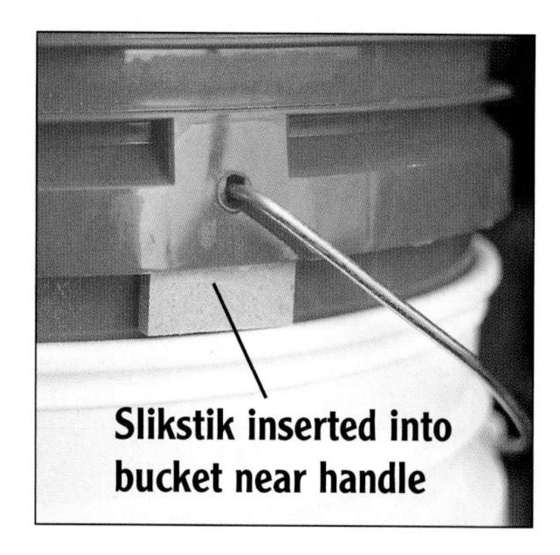

Slikstik inserted into bucket near handle

I make my slikstiks out of scrap hardboard using a template (shown below). They can also be made from metal or plastic. I'm able to make 20 slikstiks in just about as many minutes. If they are made right, slikstiks should stay inserted by themselves. However, if the buckets that are "slikstuk" together are bouncing around in the back of a pickup from day to day, you may want to glue or epoxy them in place to ensure that they will not pop out.

Joel Anderson
East Falmouth, Massachusetts

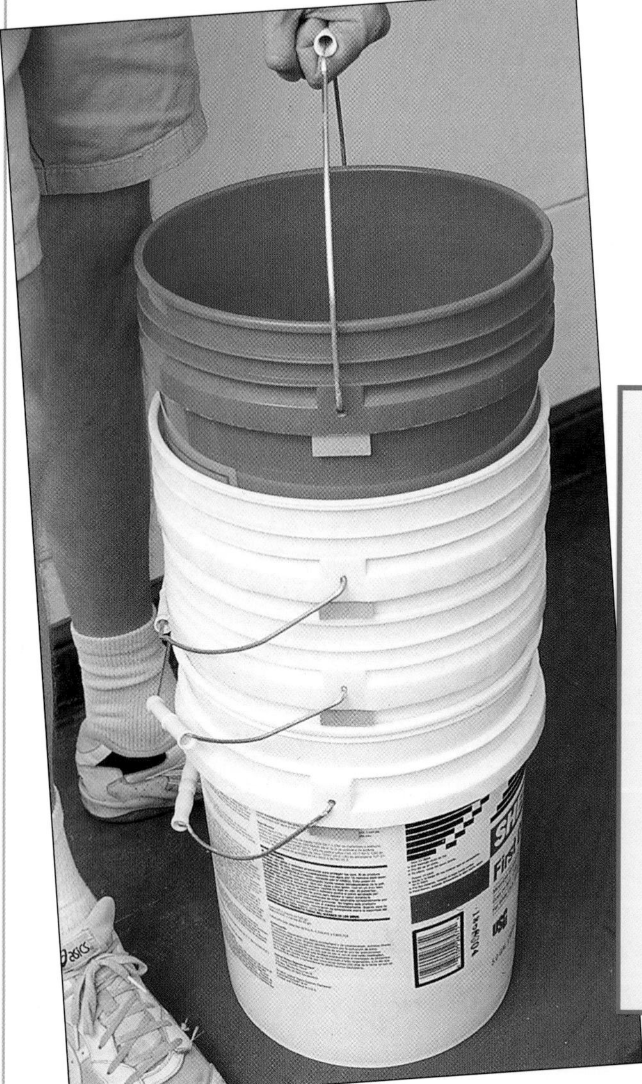

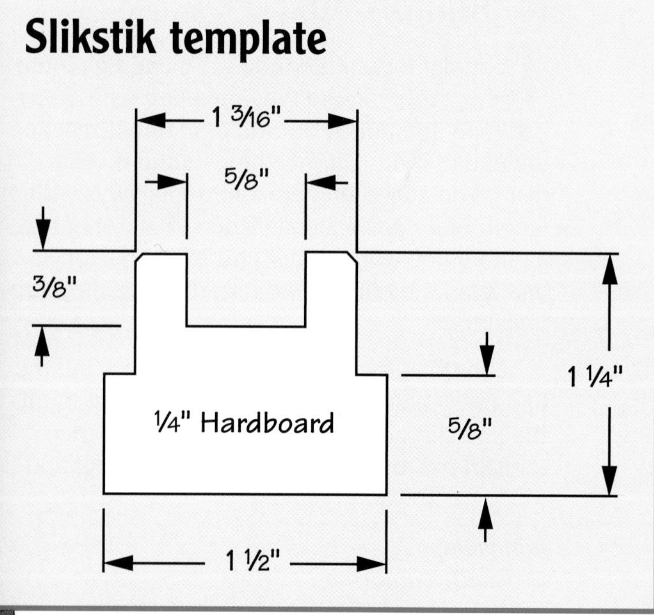

Curved sanding made easy

Here's a simple idea for a curved hand-sander—the perfect tool for smoothing rounded, odd-shaped workpieces. First, find a scrap piece of 3-in.-dia. PVC pipe and cut it to 5½ in. long. Set the fence on a band saw 2 in. from the blade and rip the PVC lengthwise. Then sand all edges of both pieces of the PVC smooth to guarantee a secure fit. Next, take a half sheet (8½ × 5½ in.) of sandpaper and wrap it around the outside of the larger piece of pipe, grit-side facing out, being sure to fold the edges over the top sides of the PVC.

Then, with their contours facing the same direction, press the smaller piece of pipe into the inside of the larger piece so that the flaps of the sandpaper are sandwiched between the two PVC sections. It is important to make sure that the ends of the pipes are flush before pressing the two pieces together, otherwise the sandpaper will hang over the edge, which might cause it to tear. If it is put together right, the PVC sections will hold the sandpaper tightly with no further clamping.

Thomas Bales
Rantoul, Illinois

SANDPAPER GRITS AND THEIR USES

Grit #	Description	Use
12/16/20/24	Very coarse	Rough work requiring high-speed, heavy-duty sanders (for example, uneven wood floors and rough-cut lumber)
30/36/40/50	Coarse	Rough carpentry
60/80/100	Medium	General carpentry
120/150/180	Fine	Preparation of hardwoods and final smoothing of softwoods
220/240/280	Very fine	Final- and between-coat sanding. Removes sanding marks left by coarser grits
320/360/400	Extra fine	Sanding between finish coats; wet sanding paints and varnishes
500/600	Super fine	Sanding metal, plastics and ceramics; wet sanding

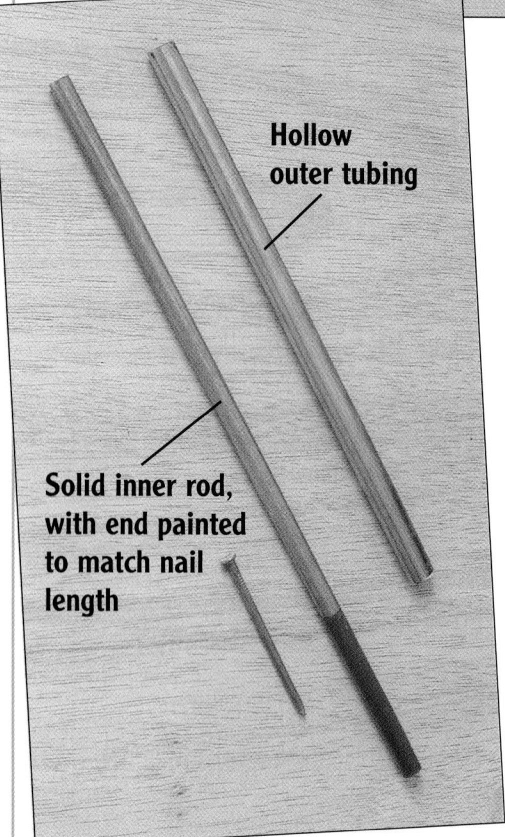

Nail driver gets you into tight spots

Sometimes nails need to be driven into tight, awkward spots, especially in remodeling projects. In many cases, using a hammer alone to drive the nails would mean marring the surrounding surfaces or damaging wiring or plumbing nearby. I've come up with a handy way to drive nails into the tightest places without damage. I simply slip a 13-in.-long piece of 5⁄16-in. metal rod inside of a 10-in.-long piece of 9⁄16-in. hollow metal tubing. I paint the end of the inner rod that extends beyond the outer rod to indicate the length of nail the nail driver will set.

To use the driver, I set the nail inside the hollow tube, slide the driving rod through the tube and onto the nailhead and hammer the painted end of the rod until the painted area meets the edge of the outer tube. When it does, I know the nail is fully driven into place. My driver allows me to drive 8d to 40d common nails smoothly.

This nail driver can be made in various sizes to suit any nail size. You can find tube and rod components in many sizes at most home centers.

William J. Chastain
Huntsville, Texas

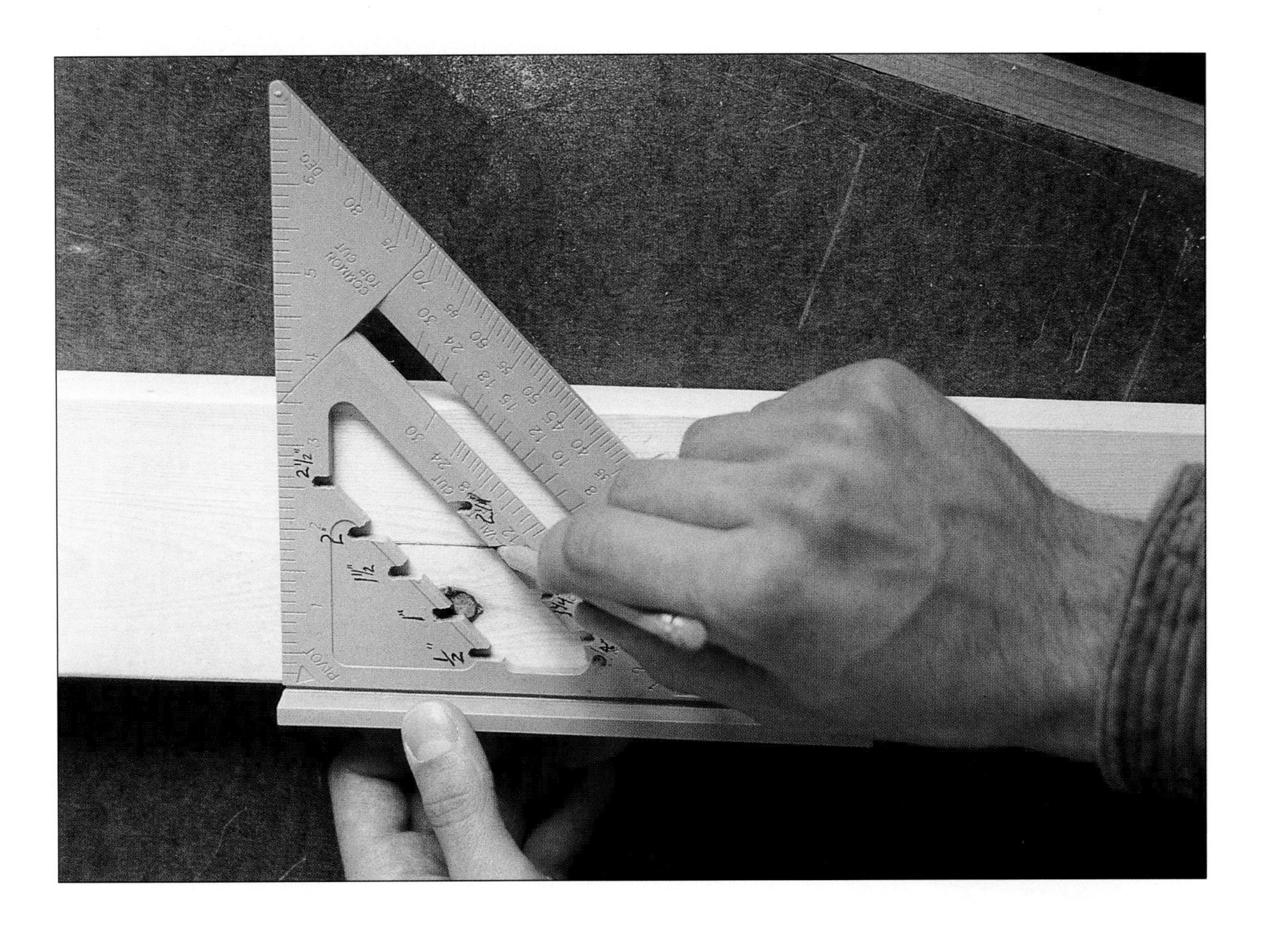

Slotted speed square doubles as marking gauge

I have found that cutting slots into my plastic speed square can be a useful way to mark pencil lines along the edges of boards, especially 2 × 4s, without measuring. I notched both sides of the cutout portion of my square in ¼-in. increments with a jig saw. One side includes measurements from ¼ in. up to 2¼ in., while the other side has slots ranging from ½ in. to 2½ in. To mark a line along a board, I just place the pencil tip in the appropriate slot and slide the square along the board's edge.

L. Brunner
Sebring, Ohio

NOMINAL VS. ACTUAL BOARD SIZES

Nominal size	Actual size
1 × 1	¾ × ¾
1 × 2	¾ × 1½
1 × 3	¾ × 2½
1 × 4	¾ × 3½
1 × 6	¾ × 5¼
1 × 8	¾ × 7¼
1 × 10	¾ × 9¼
1 × 12	¾ × 11¼
2 × 2	1¾ × 1¾
2 × 3	1½ × 2½
2 × 4	1½ × 3½
2 × 6	1½ × 5¼
2 × 8	1½ × 7¼
2 × 10	1½ × 9¼
2 × 12	1½ × 11¼

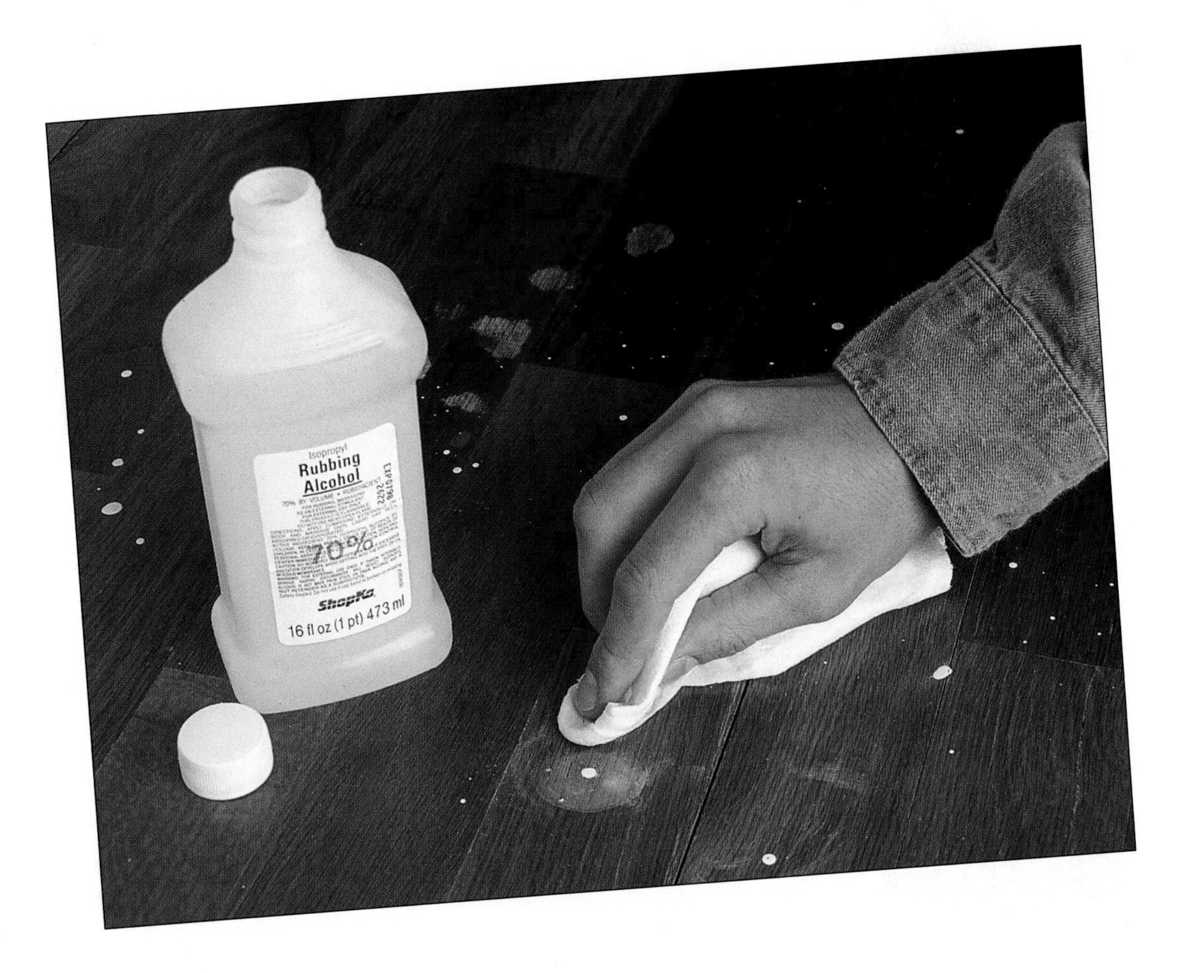

Rubbing your spills away

Here's a great tip for removing dried latex paint splatters or drops from carpets, floor coverings and woodwork. I don't like to use commercial-strength cleaners or lacquer thinner, as they can melt some surfaces (and the fumes can cause headaches and dizziness). Instead, I use regular isopropyl rubbing alcohol that we keep in our medicine cabinet. On small splatters, I use a damp rag with a little alcohol, rub it on the spill, and the spill comes right off. For a larger drop on either carpet or flooring, I pour a little alcohol on the area, blot it with a rag and rub it with another clean alcohol-dampened rag. Once the alcohol evaporates, I'm left with a clean surface and a sterile (not nauseating) smell.

Jim Dubois
Marlton, New Jersey

When you use Jim's paint cleanup tip, try it first in an inconspicuous area to be sure that the alcohol won't harm the finish beneath the spill. Follow safety precautions on the alcohol bottle label, and keep the alcohol and alcohol-dampened rags away from sparks and open flame.

Coffee can lid keeps brushes in suspension

I have solved a long-time problem that I'm sure I share with many Club Members—paintbrushes drying out. Not only have I had this problem when the brushes sit overnight without cleaning, but also while they sit between coats of paint.

I've found that coffee cans with plastic covers work quite well to keep brushes moist. I cut ½-in.-wide slits in the plastic cover with a utility knife and insert the handles of the brushes up into the slits from the bottom of the cover. I push them through far enough so that when the cover is snapped into place on the can, the brushes are suspended off the bottom, which keeps the bristles from becoming bent or damaged. For oil-based paint, I fill the coffee can with 2 in. of mineral spirits. For latex paint, I use water. The liquid keeps the bristles from drying out and serves as a handy brush cleaner and storage container.

Lisle Schrecengost
Stilwell, Kansas

Safety Note

Most cleaning solvents are both toxic and flammable. Exercise caution when working with them, provide for adequate ventilation and always keep solvents beyond the reach of children.

COMMON SOLVENTS

Type	Uses	Characteristics
Lacquer thinner	Thins lacquers and epoxies; also a general cleaner and degreaser	Highly flammable, dissolves or softens many plastics
Acetone	Cleans and removes epoxy resins, polyester, ink, contact cement	Dissolves or softens many plastics, cement and fiberglass
Mineral spirits (Turpentine)	Thinning and removal of oil-based paint, varnish, enamel and stain	Also called "paint thinner" or "gum spirits"
Solvent alcohol	Thins shellac and shellac-based primers; also good for cleaning external plastic computer parts	Soluble in water and other alcohols; should not be used with oil or latex paints, stains or varnishes
Rubbing alcohol	General cleaner, specifically used on tape recorder heads and computer disk drives	Soluble in water and other alcohols; a good disinfectant; also removes latex paint drops (see tip, opposite page)

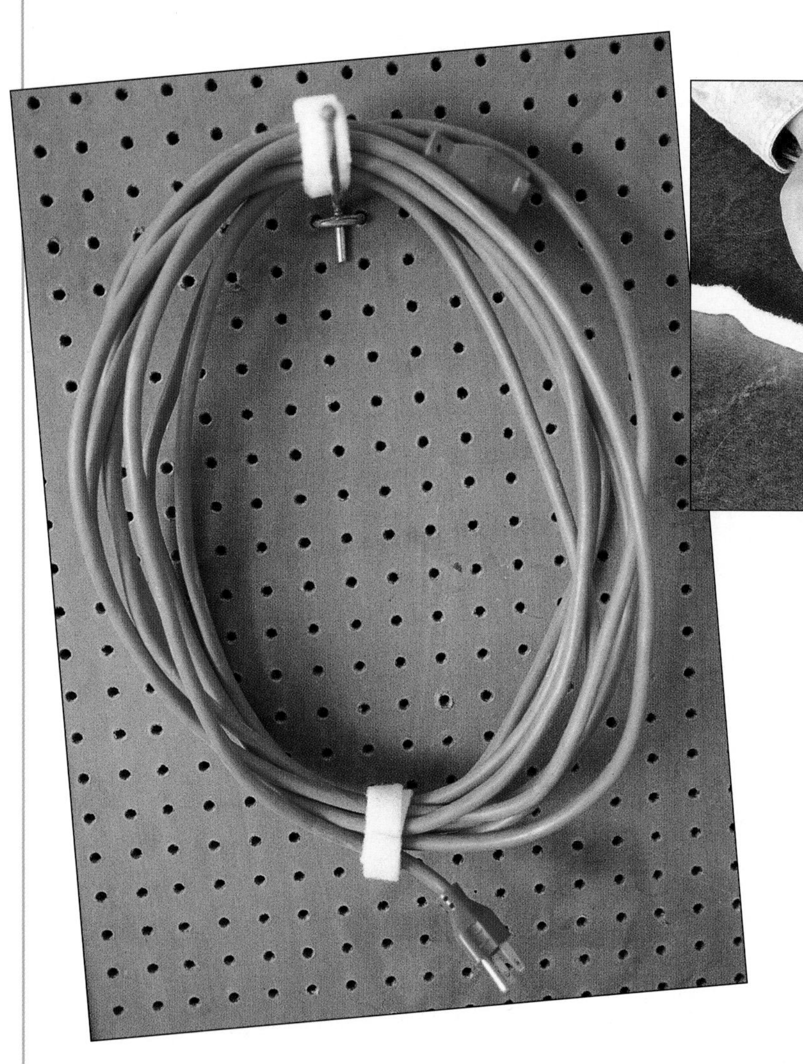

No more extension cord tangles

We all know how easily extension cords can tangle, even after they've been coiled neatly. To avoid this problem, I buy Velcro tape in 8-ft. lengths with adhesive backing. I cut a length of both the fuzzy and hooked tape long enough to wrap around the girth of my extension cord when it is fully wound up. I remove the tape covering the adhesive backing from both pieces and press the two pieces together, back-to-back. To use the strap, simply wrap it around the extension cord and press the hook-and-loop material together. I use one strap around the top of the cord loop, and the other around the bottom. For longer, thicker extension cords, you may need a few extra wraps.

Shantara Gabriel Ford
Santa Fe, New Mexico

EXTENSION CORDS

Length	Gauge	Max. amps
25 ft.	18	10
25 ft.	16	13
25 ft.	14	15
50 ft.	18	5
50 ft.	16	10
50 ft.	14	15
75 ft.	18	5
75 ft.	16	10
75 ft.	14	15
100 ft.	16	5
100 ft.	12	15
125 ft.	16	5
125 ft.	12	15
150 ft.	16	5
150 ft.	12	13

Club Note

To ensure that your power tools run safely and at peak performance, be sure that the tool you are using does not exceed the amperage rating of the extension cord. See the chart above to pick the proper gauge cord for the tool amperage and length of cord you need.

Make rubber washers at home for pennies

Sometimes you need rubber or plastic washers for a project, but the size you need is not always readily available at home. I've come up with an easy jig for making my own homemade rubber washers, any size I need.

To make my jig, you'll need a block of scrap hardwood, a wood-boring bit that matches the outside diameter of the washer you need, a band saw, some rubber or plastic tubing (preferably thick-walled rubber) and a sharp kitchen knife.

For ½-in. to ¾-in.-dia. washers, I select a small block of 2 × 2-in. hardwood scrap approximately 3 in. long. For larger washer diameters, I use a 3 × 3-in. scrap block that is about 4 in. long. Bore a hole lengthwise through the block. Check the fit of the tubing in the hole, making sure that it slides into the hole with little resistance but so that the fit is not sloppy.

Saw across the wood block parallel to the block face all the way across the hole opening, stopping the cut just after the hole. Cut the slot about ⅜ in. in from the face of the block to prevent the slotted end of the block from breaking off during use.

To use the jig, insert the tube into the hole so it clears the knife slot by the thickness of the washer you need. Take a sharp kitchen knife, insert it into the slot and slice back and forth through the rubber hose. The result should be a rubber washer with clean, parallel faces. After a little practice, you'll be able to cut washers as thin as 1⁄16-in. wide or as wide as you need with the same jig.

Bernard Harris,
Indianapolis, Indiana

After drilling the tube hole through the wood block, cut a slot parallel to the face of the block, the full diameter of the hole. The slot serves as a guide for a knife when cutting washers to size.

Suction cup idea is on the level

I put suction cups on one side of my 4-ft., 6-ft. and 8-ft.-long levels when I'm doing work on finished walls. The suction cups stick the level to most wall surfaces so I don't have to hold the level when I'm scribing level lines or hanging trim. Not only is this a helpful way to level by freeing up your hands, but it's also a convenient way to keep the tool close by. I've found that 4-ft. and 6-ft. levels need two suction cups in order to hang securely, while an 8-ft. level is better held with three suction cups. The bigger the suction cups, the stronger the hold will be.

Editor's Note: For best suction cup adhesion to wall surfaces, be sure walls are clean, flat and preferably with a glossy finish. Then moisten the suction cups with water first.

Rick Kraus
Upper Sandusky, Ohio

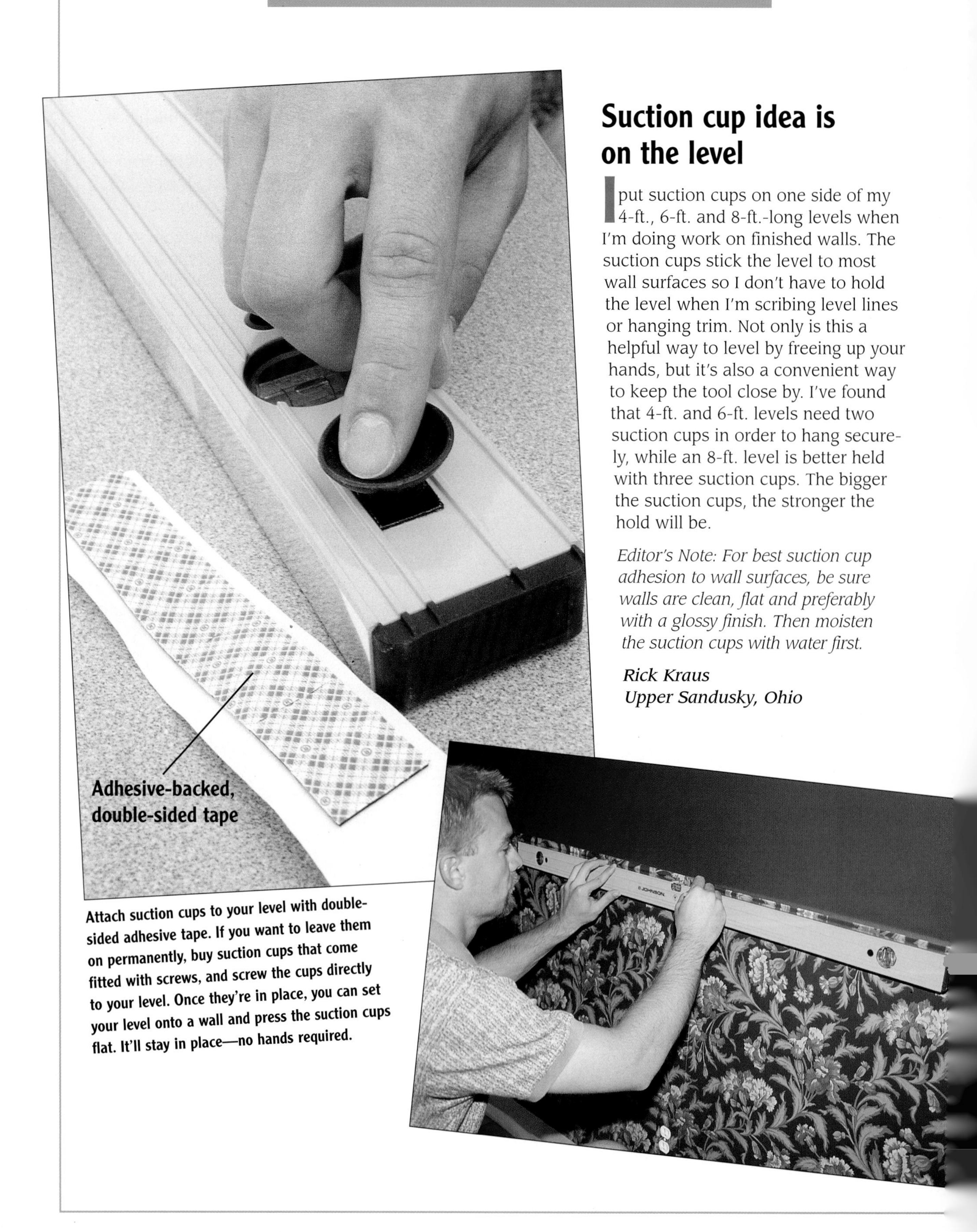

Attach suction cups to your level with double-sided adhesive tape. If you want to leave them on permanently, buy suction cups that come fitted with screws, and screw the cups directly to your level. Once they're in place, you can set your level onto a wall and press the suction cups flat. It'll stay in place—no hands required.

For easy shop-vac cleanout, cut a slit for the hose opening in a trash can liner. Set the liner into the vacuum canister, fit the slit around the hose inlet and overlap the sides of the bag outside the canister before you attach the lid. To empty your shop vac, simply pop the lid and close up and remove the bag.

Trash can liners make shop-vac cleanup a cinch

One way I've found to make workshop cleanup easier is to put a trash can liner into my shop vacuum canister. This way, you can empty the vac without having to lift and dump the entire vacuum. Most regular-size kitchen plastic garbage bags will fit into a shop vacuum. Wrap the top of the liner over the sides of the vacuum and secure the motor housing lid. This will seal the bag into place and provide more of a handle when it comes time to dispose of the contents. If your vacuum has a hose attachment mounted in the canister, cut a hole in the liner to create an opening for the hose. The liner can be secured around the inlet with tape, if needed, for reinforcement.

Paul Payne
Hollywood, Maryland

Taping first gets right to the point

For professional-looking tuck-pointing repairs every time, I use this helpful hint: Cover brick faces with either masking or duct tape before applying mortar into the joints, then remove the tape before the mortar cures. This way, the tape keeps the mortar in the joints where it belongs—not on the brick faces, which are a real mess to clean up later.

Editor's Note: Although our photos don't show it, we strongly advise that you wear chemical-resistant gloves whenever you work with wet mortar. The lime it contains can be caustic to skin. If gloves aren't available, use a joint strike—not your fingertips—to smooth mortar joints (See chart below right) and wash any mortar off your skin thoroughly with soap and water.

Mitchell Mitnick
Lake Hopatcong, New Jersey

Club Note

Here's a list of tools you'll need when tuck-pointing:

Tool	Purpose
Mortar rake or cold chisel	Scrapes out old mortar joints
Tuck-pointing tool	Loads mortar into joints
Drywall hawk	Keeps fresh mortar close at hand
Joint strike	Smooths wet mortar joints

Use shampoo for longer brush life

A good paintbrush deserves good care. One way to treat high-quality brushes right is to occasionally wash them in shampoo that comes with conditioner added. This is a fast, cheap and simple way to extend the life of expensive brushes. Not only will the shampoo thoroughly clean the brushes, it also conditions and softens the bristles much like it does for hair. We all know what a difference soft bristles can make when painting. Using this tip, it's almost like I'm using a new brush every time I paint. For what some paintbrushes cost these days, it's worth a little shampoo now and then to help them last longer.

Mark Justice
Memphis, Tennessee

PAINTBRUSH BRISTLE TYPES

Bristle type	Uses	Characteristics
Light natural	Oil-based varnish, clear stains and urethanes	Best for extra-smooth surfaces where a fine finish is desired
Dark natural	Oil-based dark stains and enamel paints	Best for smooth to semi-rough surfaces, particularly exterior
Fine polyester	Latex and water-based finishes	Leaves fewer brush marks while providing one-coat coverage
Nylon/polyester blend	Latex and water-based finishes	Value priced and holds more paint, but may not give one-coat coverage

Scrap-built sawhorses carry more than their weight

There are times when I have ¾-in.-thick plywood scraps left over from subflooring jobs that used to go to waste. Since I'm always in need of a good set of sawhorses, I've devised a simple sawhorse plan that now puts my scrap plywood to good use.

For the ends, I start with plywood pieces that are about 30 in. long and cut them so that they are 2 ft. wide at the bottom and taper at both sides to about 1 ft. at the top. I make angled cuts from the bottom corners of each leg that meet in the center, to form pointed feet on the legs (pointed feet provide more stable footing on uneven surfaces). In the top of each leg, I cut a ¾-in.-wide slit that is 3 in. long. This is where the crosspiece sits and interlocks with the legs. I cut the crosspiece to be 4 ft. long by about 1 ft. wide. Cut another set of ¾-in.-wide, 6-in.-long slits in the crosspiece about 10 in. from either end of the crosspiece at 15° angles, in toward the top.

Setting up the sawhorses is easy: Simply lock the crosspiece into the legs by sliding the cutouts together.

I've been a carpenter for more than 20 years, and I've never had these sawhorses fail to hold the weight I put on them. Plus, they come apart easily for storage. I've been on many jobs where a customer wouldn't let me leave without first making him a set.

Jerry L. Smith
Burlington, Iowa

Tape your sleeves before you roll

If you paint much with paint rollers, you know that bits of nap from new roller sleeves end up getting trapped in the paint, which can botch up an otherwise smooth paint job. Try this tip to remedy the problem. Wrap new roller sleeves with masking tape first, then pull the tape off. All of the unwanted loose nap comes with it. Slide the roller sleeve onto the paint roller handle and you're ready to go.

Dimitrios Rizos
Flushing, New York

PAINT ROLLER NAP TYPES

Nap cover	Length (in.)	Recommended surfaces
Short	**1/4 or 3/16**	**Smooth, interior or exterior**
Medium	**3/8 or 1/2**	**Semi-smooth, interior or exterior**
Long	**3/4**	**Semi-rough, interior or exterior**
Extra-long	**1 or 1 1/4**	**Extra-rough, exterior only**

Tees give new twist to old screw holes

One of the most useful and appreciated tips I've ever learned involves golf tees. It's not new, but it's definitely worth knowing. When you're hanging doors and need to replace hinges, the screw holes may be stripped or larger in the old hinge than you need for the new one. To remedy the problem, insert a golf tee until it fills the full depth of the hole. If the tee is too thick for the existing hole, pare it to size with a utility knife. Then dab wood glue on the tee and tap it into the hole. Once the glue dries, cut the tee flush with the door surface and sand it smooth. Drill a pilot hole for the new screw and drive the screws in as usual. The fit will be tight and the fix permanent.

Recently, I've discovered that golf tees also work well to fill in holes in drywall left by picture-hanger hardware. Follow the same procedure to install them in wallboard and cover the plug with spackling compound. Feather the compound out, let the area dry thoroughly and sand it smooth.

Golf tees provide a great "quick fix" material for the home handyman. Not only are the tees cheap, but they satisfy a number of handyman hole filling needs.

Gerry Gulick
Raleigh, North Carolina

Keep your fasteners organized and portable with this handy can tote. It's especially convenient for projects requiring larger quantities of more than one kind of fastener, like deck building.

Hardware tote is in the can

Everybody knows the old tin can trick for storing nails, screws and small hardware parts. It wasn't enough however, just to have all those items neatly organized in my workshop. What happens when you have a job to do away from the shop and you need to take more than one storage can with you? Not only does it take a few extra trips, but you also risk dropping a can, which is always a big mess.

To make nails, screws and other fasteners more portable, try my handy hardware tote. First, cut the handle to shape from a scrap piece of ¾-in.-thick plywood. I make my handles 12 in. long and about 4 in. tall. In the middle at the top, I make an oval-shaped handle with the center cut out for carrying.

Screw two evenly spaced rows of 46-oz. juice cans to either side of the handle with machine screws and washers (two screws and washers per can). You may want to use machine bolts and nuts, fastening each can completely through the handle. Now you can have an ample supply of fasteners wherever you need them, and they're always in order.

John Dougherty
Deerfield, New York

To get the best results from John's tote, select cans that are sturdy enough to handle the hardware you plan to carry. For heavier fasteners, you may need to use smaller cans to keep the weight manageable. As an added support measure, wrap the outside of the tote with duct or other strong packing tape.

Workshop Secrets

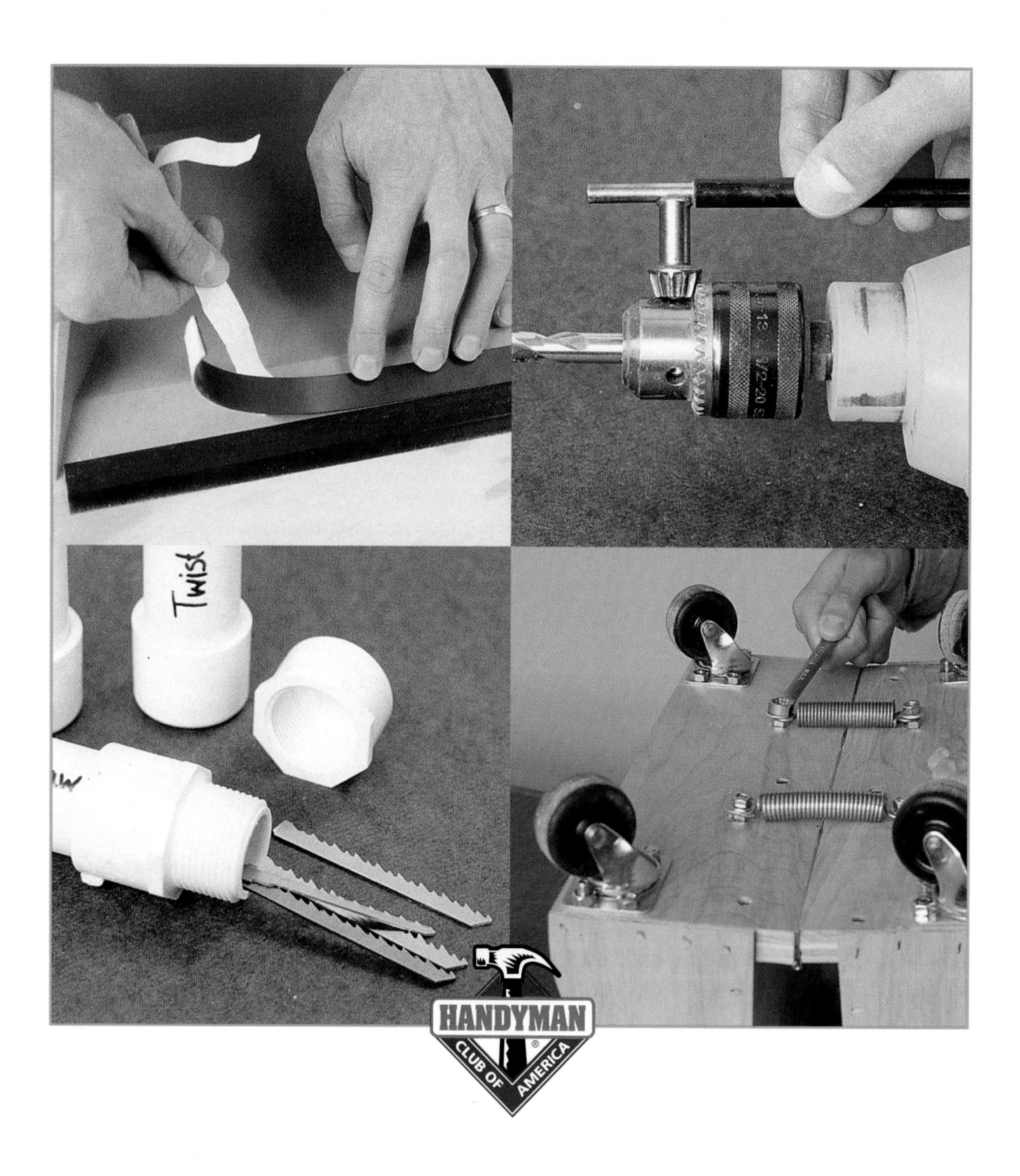

Power always at arm's reach

Because I was always tripping over the extension cords that ran along the floor to my island workbench, I designed this "retractable" extension cord. It consists of a 10-ft. length of ¾-in.-dia. thinwall conduit curved to 90° at both ends and attached to the rafters in my shop, through which I've run a triple plug extension cord. I positioned the conduit so that one end extends over my workbench and the other end reaches the wall directly above a wall outlet. I clipped off the male end of the extension cord plug (the end that plugs into an outlet) and ran the cord from the bench through the conduit, looping the extra cord at the wall. I installed a replacement plug on the cord at the wall end.

Now, when I need more extension cord at the workbench I simply reach up and pull it down from the ceiling through the conduit. When I want to store the cord up and out of the way of the workbench, I retract the extension cord at the wall by again pulling it back through the conduit. Problem solved—no more cords on the floor to catch me up.

Editor's Note: Use grommets in the ends of the conduit to keep sharp edges from cutting the extension cord.

Donald Luther
Sidney, Ohio

Conduit end with triple plug over workbench

Top-down storage

Here's an easy way to keep your wood filler, window glazing, paint, varnish or anything stored in cans from developing crust on top inside the can: Store the cans upside down. This way, the crust still forms, but it forms on the bottom of the contents of the can instead of the top. When I'm ready to use whatever it is I've stored, I make sure not to shake the can when I'm turning it right-side up. Instead, just remove the top and stir to keep whatever crust has developed on the bottom of the can. Be sure that you completely pound the lids on or screw the caps on tightly before inverting the cans. (As you can see in the photo, *Plastic Wood* already knows this tip—they label their cans with the lid on the bottom.)

James Springer
Columbia, Tennessee

Get a handle on your drill chuck keys

My chuck key extension is a great help for handymen or handywomen with arthritis. Extending the handle increases the leverage you sometimes need to release or tighten drill bits. It's simple to make using an old graphite golf club shaft or other rigid tubing. First, cut a 3-in. length of tubing that fits over the handle of your chuck key. Then attach the tubing to the chuck key with epoxy.

Richard Ammiano
St. Augustine, Florida

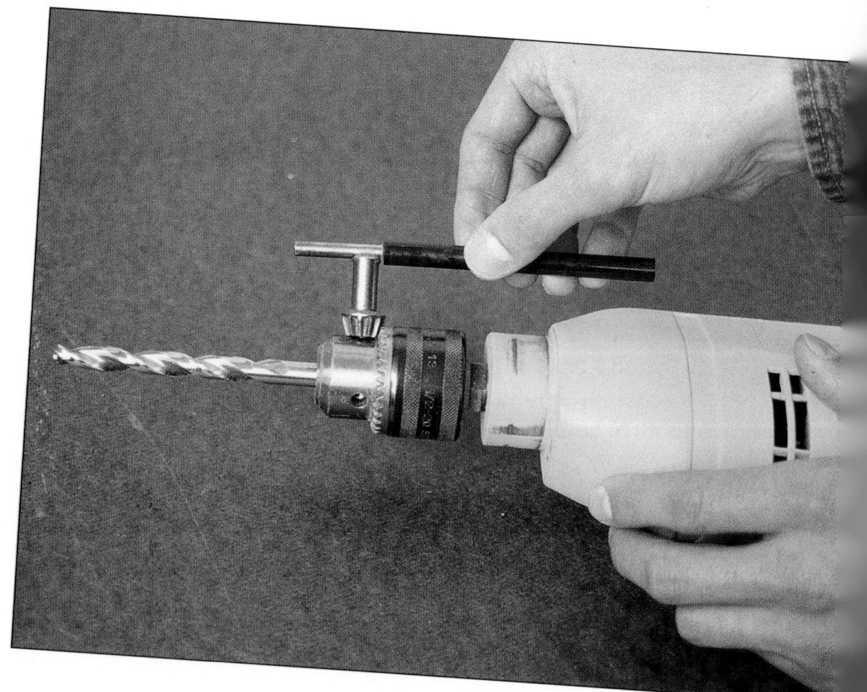

Stable storage for shop scraps

I overcame my problem of storing short but usable lengths of metal straps and threaded rods by constructing the PVC storage unit shown here. I made the containers out of 1½-, 3- and 4-in.-dia. PVC pipe, which I picked up from the remnants bin at a local hardware store. I used a fly cutter (See photo below) in my drill to cut circular grooves the same diameter as the PVC pipes 1 in. deep into a 2-in.-thick wooden base. I chose oak to create a heavy base for the storage unit. The pipes sit snugly in the grooves in the base, which keeps them from tipping over and spilling their contents.

Larry Jones
Clover, South Carolina

Larry's PVC storage system consists of scrap lengths of PVC pipe in assorted diameters that fit into a heavy wooden base. The secret to his system is that he uses a fly cutter (See photo, left) in his drill to cut circular grooves—not holes—that hold the PVC pipes in place. The fly cutter bit is the same width as the thickness of the PVC pipe walls, so the pipe sections fit snugly into their grooves in the base.

STANDARD PVC PIPE DIMENSIONS

Inside dia.	Outside dia.	Circumference
½	⅞	2¾
¾	1⅛	3½
1	1⅜	4⁵⁄₁₆
1¼	1⅝	5⅛
1½	1⅞	6
2	2⅜	7½
3	3⅜	10½
4	4⅜	14

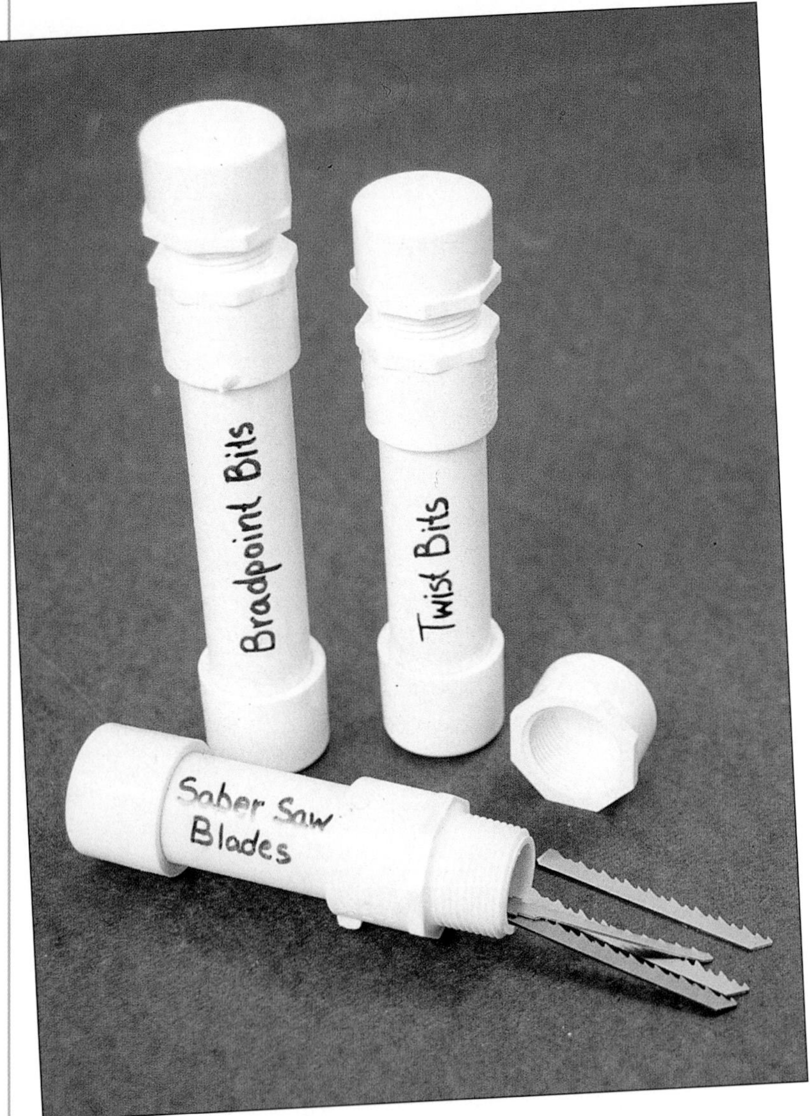

PVC bit and blade caddies

Here's an inexpensive and durable solution to store your drill bits. First, glue an end cap to one end of a length of 1-in.-dia. PVC pipe. Cut the pipe 1 in. longer than the longest bit or blade you need to store. Then solvent-glue a threaded fitting to the other end of the pipe so you can screw on a threaded cap. You can find all of these PVC parts wherever PVC pipe is sold.

I mark my bit containers for different types of shop bits, like brad-point, twist and spade drill bits, or jig saw (saber saw) blades. This way, I don't have to hunt for a specific bit type in a jumble of bits—one container holds each kind. Longer and larger diameter PVC containers can be used to store other shop tools like wood chisels, wrenches or screwdrivers.

Alton Mickle
Birmingham, Alabama

COMMON DRILL BIT DIAMETERS

Bit type	Range of diameters
Twist	1⁄64 to 1 in.
Spade	1⁄4 to 1½ in.
Brad-point	1⁄8 to 5⁄8 in.
Masonry	1⁄8 to 1½ in.
Forstner	1⁄4 to 2⅛ in.

JIG SAW BLADE SELECTION CHART

Task	Material	Length	Pitch
Fast, rough carpentry	Wood	4 in.	6 tpi
General purpose	Wood	4 in.	8 tpi
Smooth finish	Wood	4 in.	10 tpi
Extra-smooth finish	Wood	3 in.	12-14 tpi
Light metal	Metal	3 in.	12-14 tpi
Thick metal	Metal	3 in.	24 tpi

Set up shop anywhere

Occasionally I need to move my scroll saw, grinder and benchtop sanding station from place to place, depending on the location of the project I'm doing. By bolting a ¾-in.-thick piece of plywood to the bottoms of these tools and then fastening a 1 × 3-in. strip of wood to the underside of the plywood, I can clamp these tools easily into the vise of my portable workbench. This way the tools become truly portable and I have a secure worksurface that is also the right height for my tools.

Wilbert Imthurn
Aurora, Illinois

Philip's workbench "goes vertical," though the use of these cubbies set into the walls of his furnace room. Now the walls serve as work spaces, too.

Here you can see the PVC pipe outlet tube that runs from the miter saw exhaust chute to Philip's shop vacuum—a handy and inexpensive dust collection system.

Tucked-away tools

Like many fellow Club Members, my workshop is in my basement. The limited space in my basement means that the hot water heater and furnace are located in the corner of my shop. To keep these appliances free of sawdust, I enclosed them into their own room with framing, wallboard and paneling. I added a door into this "furnace room" so that I'd have ready access to the furnace and water heater for routine maintenance.

As my power tool collection grew, I added recessed cubbies into the outsides of the furnace room walls for my bench grinder and power miter saw. I used PVC drain pipe materials to make a sawdust collection system for the miter saw that empties into my shop vacuum. My design is a real workshop space saver, and the furnace and water heater stay clean.

Philip Crowl
Red Lion, Pennsylvania

Before you consider enclosing your furnace and water heater, check your local building codes for proper ventilation requirements around these appliances. Natural gas furnaces and water heaters need a source of fresh make-up air to operate properly and safely.

Sheet-goods tote

Here's a cheap and easy device that allows one person to carry large 4 × 8 sheet goods like paneling or plywood. Using a heavy-duty bungee cord, I remove one of the hook ends and insert the bungee through a 4- to 6-in. length of ¾-in.-dia. PVC pipe and replace the hook end.

To use the tote, simply hook the ends under the sheet stock and grab the PVC pipe with one hand. You'll need to guide the top of the board with your other hand when lifting and carrying to stabilize the board. With these totes, I'm able to do the work of two men all by myself.

Editor's Note: Use extra care when working in windy conditions to keep the sheet stock from catching the wind and throwing you off balance.

Dennis Farmer
Gainsville, Georgia

Club Note

This sheet goods tote works best on lighter-weight sheet stock, like plywood up to ½ in. thick or sheets of ¼-in. paneling. Be sure to use the heaviest-duty bungee cords you can find if you plan to use this tote to lift ¾-in.-thick plywood sheets or wallboard, and move one sheet at a time only. Remember, lift with your knees, not with your back.

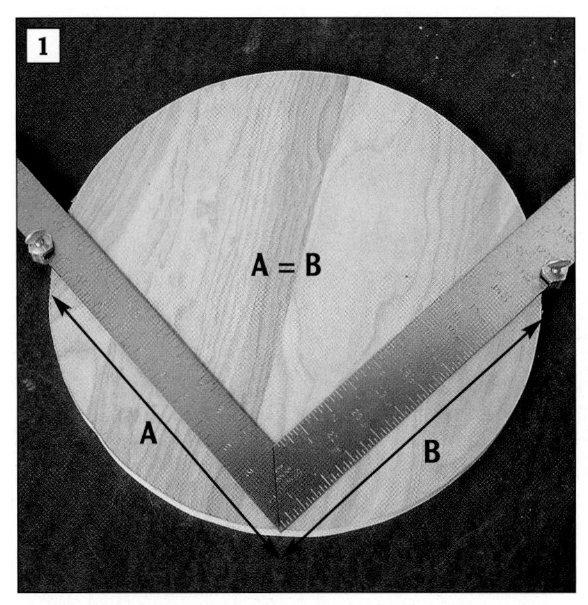

To find the center of a circle, place the corner of a carpenter's square at the circle's edge and pivot the square at this corner until the outside edges of the square's body meet the edges of the circle at equal distances from the corner.

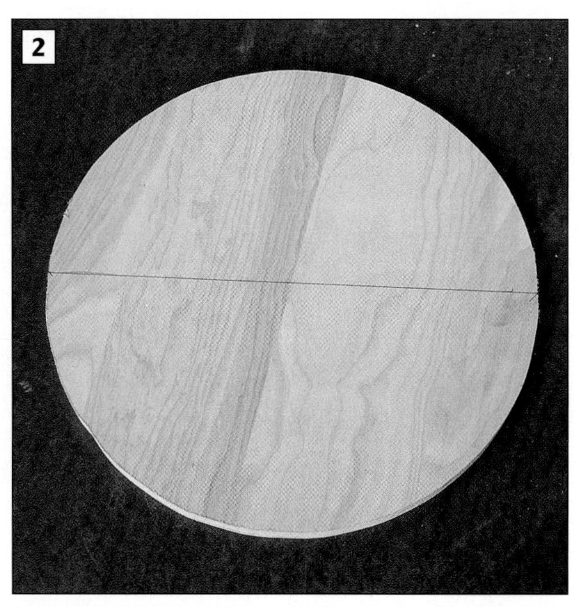

Next, connect the leg reference points you found in Step 1 by drawing a straight line across the circle.

Finding circle centers with a carpenter's square

I have seen various ways to find the center of a circle when the center is not known, but this is by far the easiest I've tried. Using a carpenter's square, line the outside corner of the tool on the edge of the circle. Keeping the corner of the square on the edge of the circle, swing the square back and forth until the outside edges on the "legs" of the square meet the circle at equal distances from the corner. Now mark the edge of the circle at these two reference points and draw a straight line to connect them. If you rotate the square about a quarter turn and repeat the first three steps, the point where the two lines cross will approximate the circle's center. The more lines you draw, the closer you'll get to dead center. Three lines usually does it for me.

Gene DeVault
Blue River, Oregon

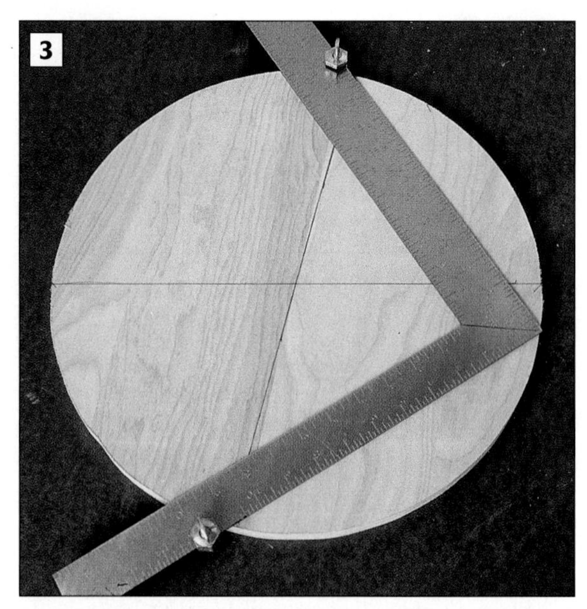

Repeat Steps 1 and 2, shifting the square about a quarter turn and drawing a new reference line across the circle. The point where the lines intersect marks the circle's center.

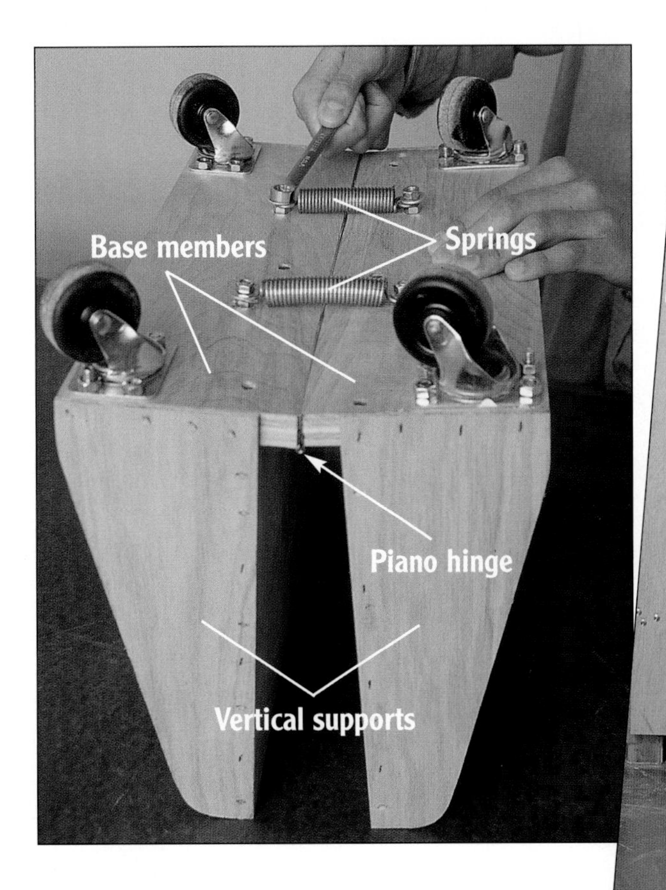

Rolling dolly for sheet goods

Need an easy-to-build dolly to move sheet stock around your shop? I've created this simple design that you can build from scrap plywood. The dolly rides on four 2¼-in. swiveling casters and consists of two vertical side supports held together with a length of piano hinge. Here's how it works: When you set a sheet of plywood between the vertical side supports, the sides tip in toward one another and hold the sheet securely on-edge. In fact, for most sheet stock, the dolly supplies all the support you need to hold the stock on-edge. When you remove the sheet from the dolly, two springs fastened across the bottoms of the vertical supports open the dolly up again, like a clam shell, so it's ready for another sheet (See photo, above).

My basic dolly design could be built larger or smaller, depending on the scraps you have available, but here are my dimensions: My finished dolly is 12 in. wide (each vertical support is 5 in. wide and sits on a 6-in.-wide base), 16 in. long and 10 in. tall. I assembled each vertical support from ¾-in. plywood fastened together with wood glue and brads. Use a piano hinge with ¾-in.-wide leaves and secure it, knuckle facing up, between the vertical supports at the bottom. Screw one caster to each corner of both vertical supports. To protect the sheet stock while in the dolly, I lined the inside faces of the vertical supports with rubber cabinet door bumpers, two on each side.

Michael Guimont
Princeton, Minnesota

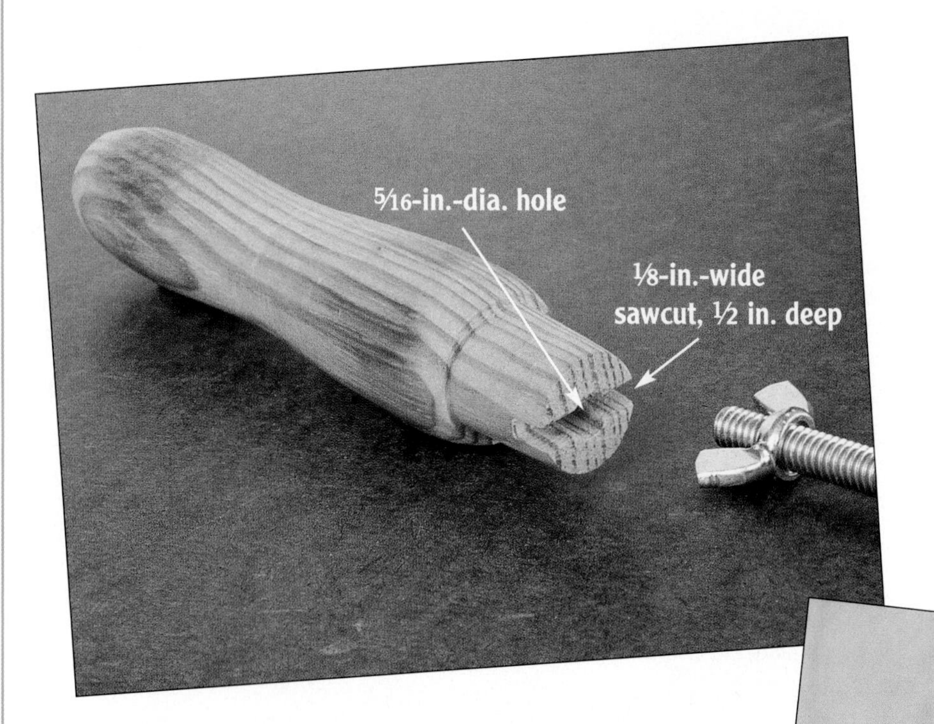

No more stubborn wing nuts

A convenient tool I created and have used for some time is this wing nut wrench. It makes loosening and tightening wing nuts on workshop tools and jigs much easier on old, tender hands and fingers. I initially used a file handle for the wrench body, but I've since turned a handle on my lathe so that it would better fit my hand and add a little thickness at the working end. You could also use a length of thick doweling or hand railing and shape it with a sander.

I drilled a 5⁄16-in.-dia. hole about 1 in. into the end of the handle lengthwise so that it would fit over a 1⁄4-in.-dia. bolt. Then I cut a 1⁄8-in.-wide slot 1⁄2 in. deep across the end of the handle in order to fit over the wings and hub of a wing nut. To use the wrench, slip it over a wing nut and align the wings of the nut in the slot. Tighten or loosen the nut as needed by twisting the handle. I screwed an eye screw in the opposite end of the handle to hang it on a hook near my router table, where I use it most often.

James Perrone
Columbia, South Carolina

Get more mileage from your scroll saw blades

My scroll saw blades typically dull in the center section where they get the most use. Farther up on the blade, however, the ones I used to discard are as sharp as new. To make your scroll saw blades last longer, try this tip: Once a blade gets dull, cut a piece of flat, smooth ¾-in.-thick plywood that matches the size of the scroll saw table. Then make a saw cut for the blade from the edge of the plywood to the center, slide the plywood table into position and clamp it to the saw table. By adding the plywood insert on top of your saw table, you'll raise the cutting area of the saw blade and make use of part of the blade that is still sharp. The plywood can be reinstalled and used whenever you need it, and your blades will give you much more service!

Al Wubker
O'Fallon, Missouri

SCROLL SAW BLADE SELECTION CHART

Task	Type	Gauge	Pitch
General cutting	Scrolling	#5	15 tpi
Finer cutting without tearout	Reverse-tooth fret	#7	11.5 tpi
Fast, finer scrollwork	Scrolling	#7	12 tpi
Tight curves	Spiral-tooth	#2	41 tpi
Fast cuts	Fret	#9	11.5 tpi

Matthew's rotary carving tool workstation uses a slitted clamping block beneath the worksurface (See photo, below) to hold the tool in position. The whole worktable can be held securely in a workbench vise.

"No hands" shaping

I built a worktable to hold my rotary carving tool, which frees up my hands for cutting and shaping small parts. The worktable is composed of two parts—a flat worksurface with a hole bored through the center for the rotary tool, and a slitted clamping block screwed under the worksurface that holds the rotary tool in place. To use it, I slide the tool through a hole in the clamping block and up through the hole in the worktable. Then I tighten a bolt that runs through the clamping block, which secures the rotary tool in position. I made the clamping block beneath the worksurface large enough to allow me to clamp the worktable in my workbench vise.

Matthew DeCosta
Assonet, Massachusetts

Attached to the underside of the worksurface, the slitted clamping block is outfitted with a bolt and nut to pinch the rotary tool in position. To change the bit height above the worksurface, loosen the nut and slide the tool up or down. Then retighten the bolt.

Club Note

If you use longer, heavier nails and screws in your shop and find that these items aren't caught as easily on the magnetic strip, attach a second magnetic strip next to the first. This will provide a wider surface area to catch those larger fasteners.

Magnetic dustpans separate washers from waste

I find it helpful to attach a magnetic strip to the front edge of my workshop dustpan (See photo, above). Inexpensive rolls of magnetic strip with adhesive backing are commonly available at variety stores. When you fill up a dustpan with shop debris, screws, nails and other small steel hardware items like washers and nuts will be attracted to the magnetic strip, while sawdust and dirt will fall into the trash (See photo, right). This is a quick way to recover and save fasteners and parts that you can still use without having to sift through the dust pile on the shop floor or in your trash can.

Steve Munro
Eaton Rapids, Michigan

Woodworking Secrets

Tape takes stress out of band saw blade changes

I used to have problems installing the blades on my band saw, especially the narrow ones. It was hard to keep the blade from slipping off of one guide wheel while I tried to position it around the other wheel. In the process of fumbling with the unwieldy, and usually new, sharp blade, I was putting myself at risk of getting cut.

Here's my simple solution to the problem: Take two pieces of masking tape and secure the blade to the top wheel. This holds the blade in position while you center it on the bottom wheel and tighten it. Once the blade is tightened, remove the tape and you're ready to go. I have excellent results replacing band saw blades using this method—and no more frustration.

Clifford Schweiger
Brooklyn Park, Minnesota

Safety Note

Be sure to remember to unplug your band saw, or any power tool, before making blade changes. Also, wear eye protection when uncoiling new band saw blades—the blades are under tension in the package and can spring open, causing injury.

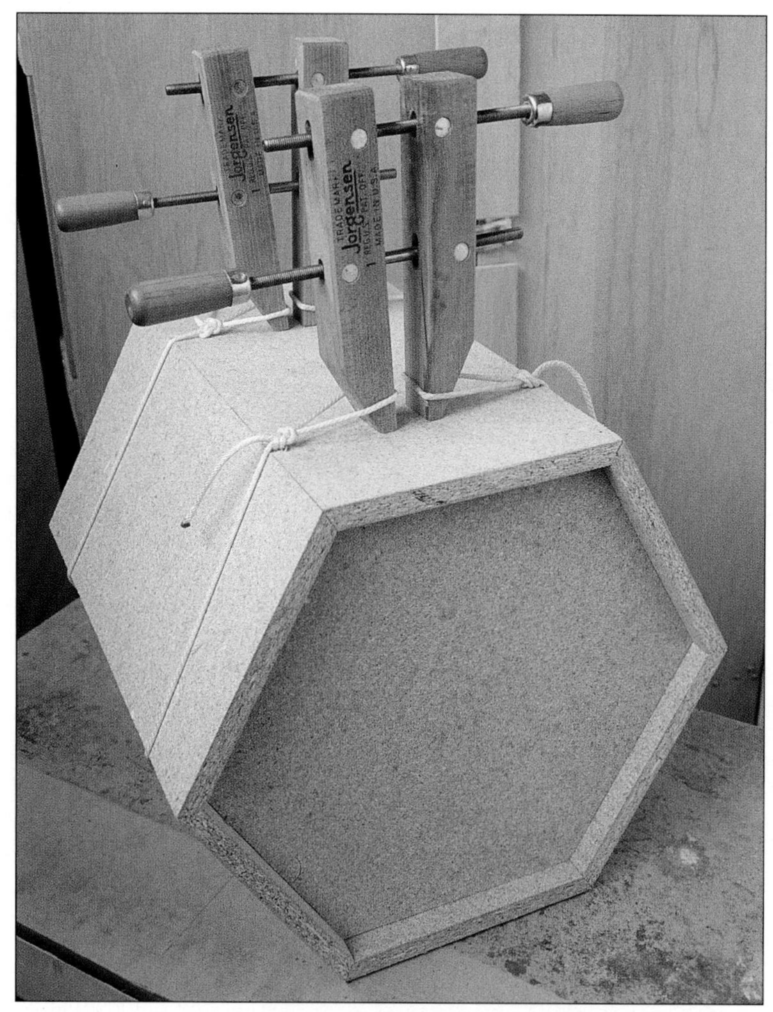

Get ahold of odd-shaped glue-ups using Robert's shop-built strap clamps. All that stands between you and tight glue joints is a couple lengths of nylon rope and some wood-screw clamps.

Pressure from all sides

I have built stereo speaker cabinets in the past that have been too large or awkward for pipe clamps to hold them tightly while gluing, drilling and screwing. My speaker cabinets frequently are designed in non-square shapes like pyramids or have multiple sides. In these cases, pipe clamps aren't much help.

I've developed my own version of a strap clamp to solve this problem. Here's how: Take a length of nylon rope and tie a 6- to 8-in. loop on either end. The length of the rope, including the loops, should be 2 to 4 in. shorter than the circumference of the cabinet. Then, using the type of machinist's C-clamp that has closing jaws (not just contact pads) or a wood-screw clamp, I wrap the rope around the cabinet, place a loop over each jaw of the clamp (in the open position) and tighten. As the clamp tightens, so does the rope, applying even pressure around the entire cabinet.

Robert Galler
Rio Rancho, New Mexico

Straight-to-the-point finishing

When I make cabinet doors and shelves, I like to be able to apply the finish coat on both sides of the workpiece without waiting for one side to dry first. To solve the problem of how to hold up the workpiece without damaging the wet finish on one face while I finish the other face, I drill countersunk holes through the center of 1 × 2 × 2-in. scrap wood blocks and screw 2-in. wallboard screws into as many of the blocks as I need. After finishing one face of a workpiece, I put three or four blocks on my workbench with the screw points facing up. Then I carefully set the door or shelf I am finishing with its wet side touching the screw tips and proceed to finish the other face. The screw points provide just enough support for a cabinet door or shelf and do not damage the finish as it dries. *Editor's Note: To keep your still-wet finish from sagging when you flip the workpiece over, apply each coat as thinly and evenly as possible.*

R. B. Gostomski
Owen, Wisconsin

TOPCOATS AND DRYING TIMES

Topcoat	Drying time
Oil-based polyurethane	Three hours to touch; 24 hours to normal use
Water-based polyurethane	Two hours between coats; three hours to handling
Lacquer	Two to four hours
Shellac	Fifteen minutes to touch; two hours to re-coat
Tung oil	Eight to 10 hours for normal use; 24 hours between coats
Danish oil	Twenty-four hours for normal use; 72 hours before final coat
Linseed oil	Twelve to 18 hours

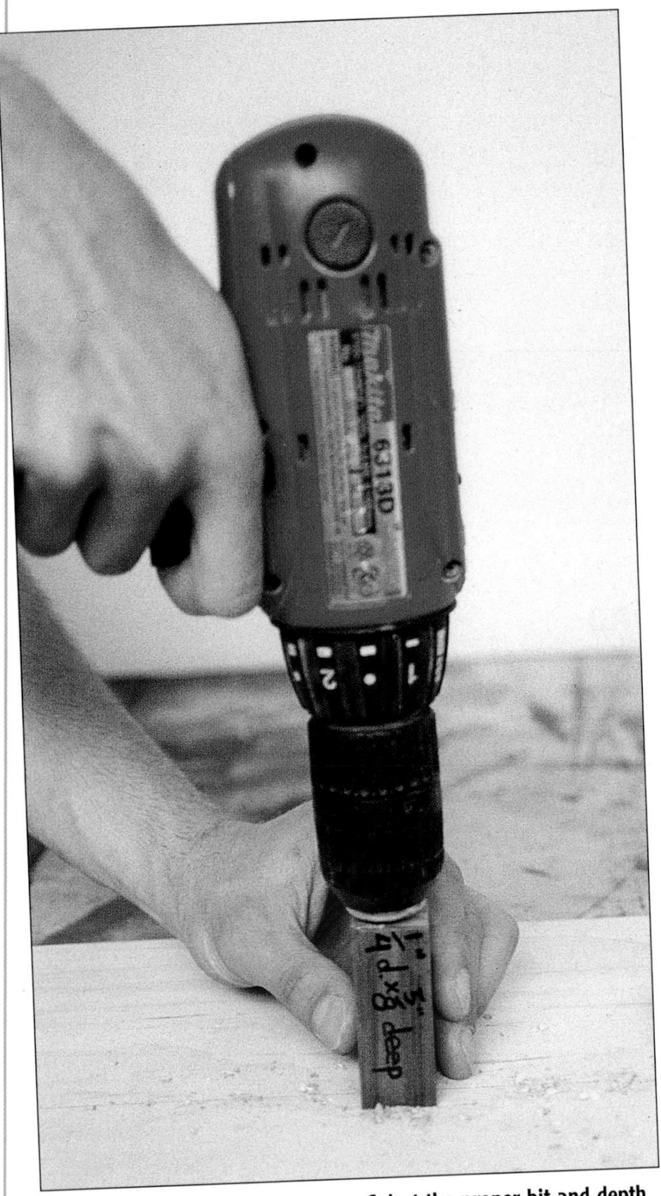

Dean's depth stops are easy to use. Select the proper bit and depth stop and install the bit in the drill chuck. Slip the block over the bit and measure the length that the bit extends beyond the block. Adjust the bit depth as necessary to match the hole depth you want to drill. Then hold onto the depth stop and drill your holes. The hole depths will be exactly the same, and square faces on the block will ensure that the holes are perpendicular to the face of the workpiece.

Shop-made drill guides

When I needed to drill some accurate holes for bookcase shelf pegs but didn't have a drill bit depth stop collar or my right-angle drill guide, I came up with a quick fix. I drilled a hole one size larger than the diameter of the hole I needed for the shelf pegs lengthwise through a short block of hardwood scrap. I then installed the correct size bit for the pegs in my drill and measured its length from the drill chuck to the bit tip. I used this measurement to determine how long to cut the block depth stop, so that when I inserted the bit through the hole in the block, it would extend beyond the block the correct depth of the shelf peg holes I wanted to drill. This way, I knew the depth stop would allow me to drill holes of the same depth quickly and easily.

Square stock with squared ends works best for a couple reasons. First, in a pinch my depth stops also serve as right-angle drill guides, provided you hold the blocks flat on your workpiece. Second, square faces on the blocks allow you to get a good grip on the depth stop to keep it from turning as you drill, which can leave burn marks on your work. Now that I have one, I prefer to use my right-angle drill guide with its adjustable depth stop for similar drilling tasks, but I'm glad I came up with this quick fix alternative when the right equipment isn't available.

Dean Hallal
Sumter, South Carolina

Club Note

As an addition to Dean's resourceful tip, we suggest you label your depth stops with both the drill bit diameter and the depth hole the block is intended to cut. Labeling will take the guesswork out of selecting the right depth stop the next time you need to drill same-depth perpendicular holes.

Short saw supports make for easy access

When sawing up a 4 × 8 sheet of plywood, I mark my cutting line with either a chalk line or a straightedge and pencil. I then place two 2 × 4s 6 in. or so apart on a level surface, such as a large worktable or on the floor. After laying the plywood on top of the 2 × 4s with the cut line aligned between the boards beneath, I saw along the line with my circular saw. I've found that this short support method works better than trying to saw the plywood on two sawhorses, because you're not supporting large and sometimes unwieldly pieces of plywood so far off of a stable surface. *One more tip:* Be sure to set your circular saw blade so that it extends no more than ½ in. below the plywood, to keep it from coming into contact with the worksurface beneath.

Jerome Moonen
Somerville, Tennessee

CIRCULAR SAW BLADE SELECTION CHART

Task	Type	Tpi (8¼-in./10-in.-dia.)*
General purpose	Combination	16-36/18-50
Trim carpentry	Crosscut	40-64/60-80
Rough carpentry	Crosscut	34-40/40-60
Smooth crosscutting	Crosscut	50-64/60-80
Rip-cutting	Ripping	16-36/18-24
Plywood and particleboard	Plywood/panel	48-64/60-80
Light metal	Metal-cutting	58-64/60-72

*Note: Tpi represents teeth per inch for either 8¼-in. or 10-in.-dia. blades

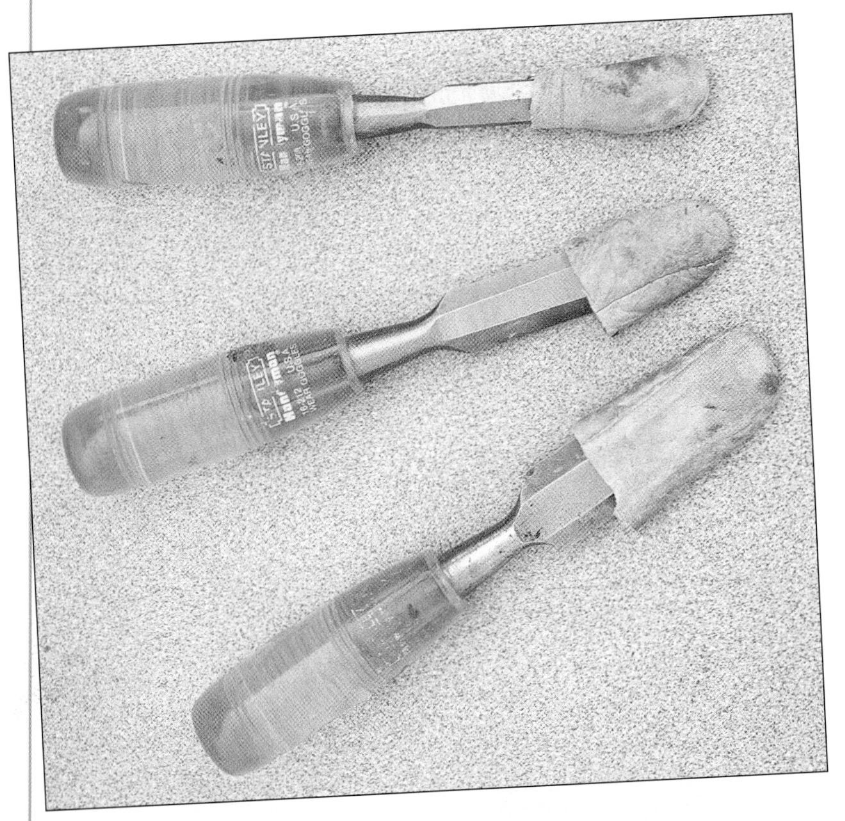

Old gloves find new life

I cut the tips off the fingers of old leather gloves and use them to cover the cutting edges of my chisels. The leather is a sturdy material that protects the chisels from accidental dings. Using these covers, my chisels stay sharper longer and I'm able to use old gloves that I would have normally just thrown away.

Linda Addison
DaCono, Colorado

A little slip ensures a tight fit

When using a belt or strap clamp, the strap has a tendency to grab on sharp corners and distort the workpiece. I've found that by putting a square of wax paper at each corner, the belt will slide smoothly over sharp edges until it is tight and the workpiece will not get distorted in the process.

John Vieth
Chicago, Illinois

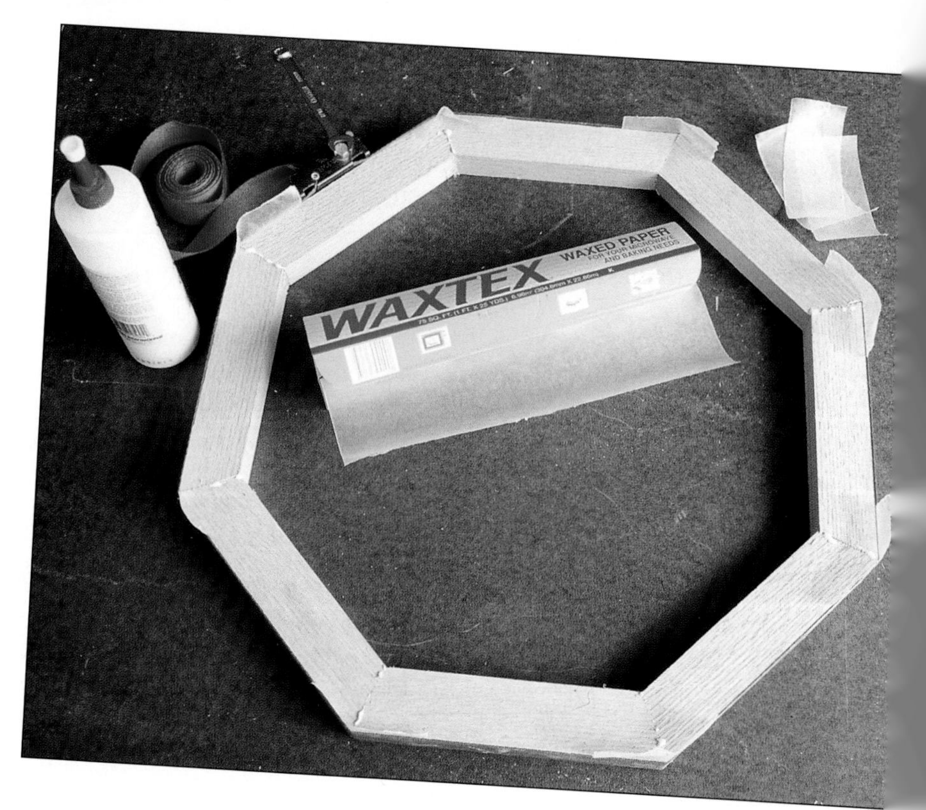

Steel wool hold-down eases the rub

I have always found it difficult to keep a steel wool pad from rolling or balling up when I'm trying to rub down new varnish between coats. Recently, I had this problem while refinishing a hardwood floor. I decided to try something different. I took a rubber 3 × 4-in. sanding block (with the sandpaper still attached) and placed the pad of steel wool on top of the sandpaper. I then used the block in the usual fashion to move the steel wool back and forth over the work. The sandpaper on the sanding block held the steel wool flat and stationary, and it did a great job of rubbing down the new varnish. In addition, keeping the steel wool pad flat seems to make it last much longer.

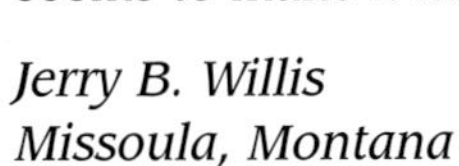

Jerry B. Willis
Missoula, Montana

STEEL WOOL TYPES AND USES

Type	Description	Uses
#3	Coarse	Removing old paint and varnish
#2	Medium coarse	Cleaning glass brick, rough metal, concrete or brick. Removing rust and dirt from garden tools, scuff marks from floors, as well as paint from molding and corners
#1	Medium	Cleaning linoleum, rubber asphalt and other resilient floors, copper pipe and fittings and automobile whitewalls
#0	Medium fine	Cleaning pots and pans. Also removes rust from metal tools
#00	Fine	Buffing final finish on painted trim. Cleaning golf clubs, screens and frames. Removing wood floor stains and old finishes from antiques (if used with finish remover)
#000	Very fine	Polishing aluminum, copper, brass and zinc. Removing minor burns from wood and leather, paint drips and splatters, rust from chrome surfaces
#0000	Super fine	Buffing woodwork, shellac and varnish (if used with wax or oil). Smoothing clear wood finishes. Cleaning delicate instruments, precision tools and glass without chemicals

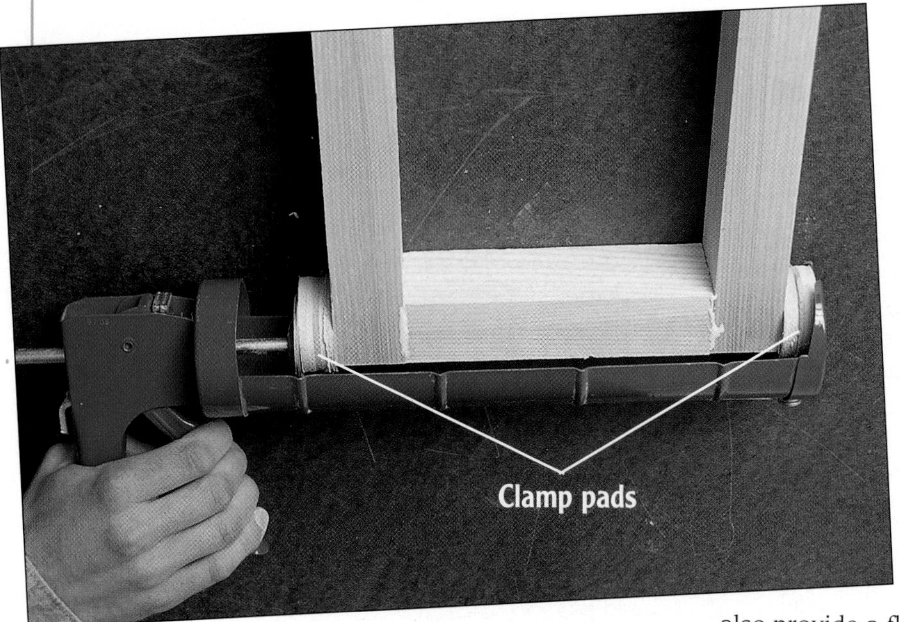

Caulk gun keeps the pressure on

A caulk gun is ideal for applying light pressure to small workpieces being glued together. I place the workpieces between two scraps of wood that serve as clamp pads, then position the assembly between both jaws of the caulk gun. The scraps not only protect the workpieces being glued, but also provide a flat surface to ensure that even pressure will be applied on both sides. By squeezing the trigger, I'm able to apply just the right amount of pressure in small increments until the assembly is held tightly and the two pieces can dry sufficiently. This is ideal for hobby projects where pipe and wooden clamps would be too large.

William Gates
Silverhill, Alabama

ADHESIVES BY TYPE AND USE

Type	Strength	Cleanup/solvent	Surfaces
White glue	Medium	Soap and water	Porous (indoor wood, paper and cloth)
Yellow glue	Medium-high	Soap and water	Porous (indoor wood, paper and cloth)
Liquid hide glue	High	Mineral spirits	Porous (indoor wood, paper and cloth); reactivates when it contacts itself
Polyurethane glue	High	Mineral spirits	Porous & non-porous (indoor/outdoor wood, metal, ceramic, stone and plastic); must be moist for activation
Construction adhesive	Very high	Mineral spirits	Indoor porous/non-porous building materials (wood, drywall, stone, brick veneer and ceramic)
Water-based contact cement	Medium-high	Soap and water	Porous & non-porous (plastic laminate, metal plywood, rubber and cloth)
Hot glue	Medium	Heat	Porous & non-porous (glass, plastic and wood)
Two-part epoxy	Very high	Acetone	Porous & non-porous (indoor/outdoor wood, metal, masonry, glass and fiberglass)
Instant glue	Very high	Acetone	Non-porous (plastic, metal, ceramic and glass)

Glue tip really cuts the mustard

The best glue container I've ever used is the lowly plastic mustard bottle. I buy larger containers of wood glue for a better price and fill my mustard bottle whenever I need something with an applicator-style tip. I fill the mustard bottle directly from my larger glue bottle. The mustard bottle applicator is designed so that even if I forget to close the top, the contents won't dry out because very little air can reach the glue. I have left my bottle open for as long as 48 hours, and the applicator still worked as if the top had been closed the entire time. The only place that glue might harden after use is on the tip, but this thin layer can be easily picked off with any sharp, pointed object.

Donald Santee
Fairport, New York

Home & Yard Secrets

Siphoning without the bitter aftertaste

If you've ever started a siphon hose by sucking on it and ended up with a mouthful of gasoline, you might appreciate my tip for siphoning without using your mouth. Take the hose and place it in whatever container you are trying to drain. Hold the other end of the hose over the container you want to fill. Instead of sucking on the end of the siphon tube to start the liquid flowing, blow compressed air across the end of the siphon tube. The compressed air passing over the end of the tube will create a low-pressure area in front of the tube, drawing fluid through it. As soon as the fluid is flowing, you can shut off the compressed air and place the tube into the container you're filling. Once you've drained all that you can by siphoning, blow air across the end of the tube again and use the other end to literally vacuum the remaining liquid from the bottom of the container that you're draining.

Dermot Madden
Bloomfield Hills, Michigan

Club Note

When using Dermot's helpful hint, we found that holding the compressor nozzle at an angle slightly less than 90° near the end of the tube works best to draw fluid up the tube. Try several angle adjustments until you get the best results from the equipment you're using. Never point the compressor nozzle into the tube, or the compressed air will force the liquid out of the container at the other end.

Mark drywall for receptacle boxes without measuring

Since I do a lot of wallboard work, I've come up with a handy tip for marking receptacle box locations. I drill a hole in each corner of a receptacle box faceplate—any switch plate cover or receptacle box cover will do. Then I drive four short machine screws through the holes I drilled so that the screw tips face out from the cover. I screw this cover to the receptacle box before I hang the wallboard. As I set the sheet of wallboard into position, the machine screws puncture the back of the wallboard and mark the exact location of the corners of the receptacle, telling me where to cut the hole in the wallboard. After I cut the receptacle box hole and set the wallboard in place, the receptacle box lines up perfectly.

Lee Potts
Canton, Ohio

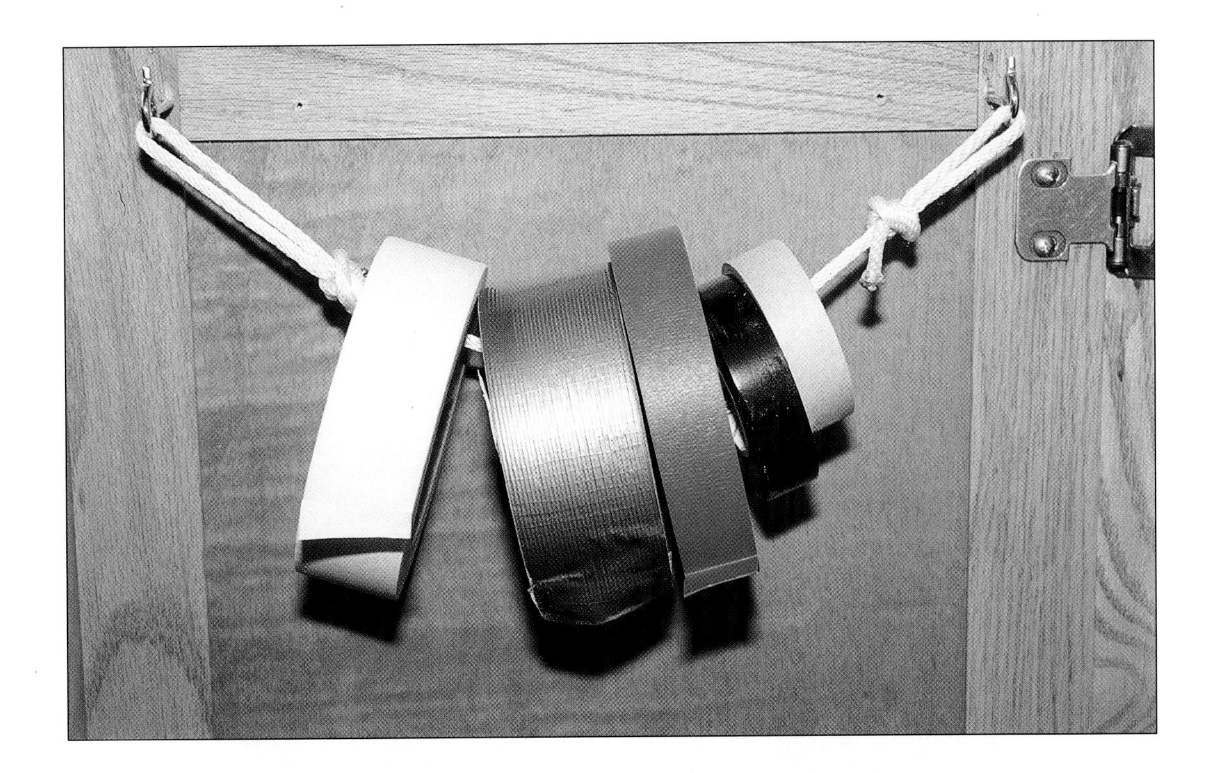

Tape on a rope

I find it helpful to have assorted household tapes in a central location. I keep mine on a string hooked to a shelf under my kitchen sink, but a cabinet door would work well, too. This method of storage takes up minimal space, and it eliminates searching through a kitchen junk drawer. I put hooks at both ends of the string so that, at most, I only have to take off a few rolls to reach a roll of tape in the middle of the string. This way, rolls of tape are easy to identify and are readily available whenever I need them.

Darla Gravatt
Lubbock, Texas

Here's the scoop: Lay tarp before you dig

The next time you're doing a landscaping project and need to pile dirt on a grassy area, lay a plastic tarp down first. The tarp will keep the dirt from settling into your grass, which makes cleanup difficult and tough on the lawn. When you remove dirt from the tarp, pull up the tarp corners, which will re-pile the dirt in the center of the tarp—it'll make shoveling easier. (Be careful to keep your shovel from puncturing the tarp as you scoop). When you're done, you'll be left with a clean grassy area beneath the tarp—no raking required.

Delbert Jessen
Minnetonka, Minnesota

Semi-automatic trash can liners

Are you always looking for the box of kitchen trash bags when trash day comes? Try this tip, and you'll never search for the trash bags again. Buy a roll of bags with perforated dividers. Drop the entire roll into the bottom of the trash can, and pull one bag up into place as usual. When the bag is full, tie it and pull the bag out of the can. The next bag will pull up into place, since it's attached to the bag that you're removing. Tear the full bag off, refit the next bag in the can, and you're ready to go again. If you buy large rolls, you won't have to search for another trash bag for a couple of hundred changes.

John Faucett
Piedmont, Alabama

For better drying, blow your hose

Here's an easy way to clean lint buildup from your dryer vent. Disconnect the vent hose from your dryer and attach the end to the nozzle of an electric leaf blower. To improve the seal, I wrap painter's tape around the hose where it fits over the blower nozzle. Be sure to also remove the screen from the vent outlet outside your home if one exists (some vents do not have a screen). Then turn on the blower. I let the leaf blower run for three to five minutes, which blows out any loose lint. I shake the vent hose as the blower runs to loosen even more lint. Reconnect the hose to the dryer and check the vent outside for any remaining blockage. Vacuum it from the outside—do not blow it back down the vent hose.

Jeff Small
Ft. Wayne, Indiana

We recommend cleaning the vent hose on your dryer regularly, especially if you have a gas clothes dryer or dry clothes often. Lint buildup in gas dryers is a potential fire hazard. You can also minimize lint buildup by keeping your run of dryer vent hose as straight as possible. Lint collects where the vent hose bends.

Handy paint holder

When I buy paint or stain that comes in a gallon-size bucket or larger, I transfer a portion of the liquid into the top section of a 1-gallon bleach bottle with the lid screwed on tightly. I cut off the bottle about 2 in. below the handle. This gives me a handle to hold onto while I paint and works well whether I'm working from the ground or on a ladder.

Editor's Note: Be sure to thoroughly wash the bleach container to remove all bleach residue before filling it with paint or stain.

Dennis Witt
Hamburg, New York

THE FIVE BASIC HOUSE PAINTS

Type	Advantages	Disadvantages	Uses
Oil-based	Good adhesion to chalky surfaces	Slow drying, strong smell	Mainly exterior or well-ventilated areas
Alkyd	Fast drying and odorless; produces tough coating	Not resistant to chemicals, solvents or corrosives	Excellent interior paint
Emulsion (Latex)	Fast drying; highly resistant to blistering and peeling	Poor adhesion to chalky surfaces	Interior and exterior at temperatures above 45°
Water-thinned	Easy cleanup	Poor adhesion to non-porous surfaces	Primarily for masonry surfaces
Catalytic	Extremely durable; highly resistant to acids, chemicals and daily wear	Two parts must be mixed; cannot be applied over other types of paint	Mainly exterior or well-ventilated areas

Add a bumper to your trimmer

To extend the life of my lawn string trimmer, I've glued an appropriate-sized metal cap (a regular 1-in.-dia. nut or washer, for example) onto the "bump knob" that extends the line on the trimmer. I made this simple modification to protect the plastic knob on the trimmer from wear and tear caused by continual banging against the ground. I hope it will make my trimmer last forever!

I. Turman
Chicago, Illinois

When using a string trimmer, protect yourself from flying bits of nylon trimming line and debris. Wear safety glasses, long pants and a shirt with long sleeves. If your trimmer is gas-powered, you may also want to consider wearing hearing protection.

Spill-proof pipe glue

I picked up this simple tip from a plumber I know. When gluing plastic pipe together, tape the solvent and primer cans together first. Both are needed to do the job anyway, and this tip makes sure that you can always find each can in order to complete the job. It also makes it harder to spill the cans—which is an awful experience when it happens, believe me!

Joseph Steen
New Albany, Massachusetts

Club Note

Solvent-welding PVC pipe

The Uniform Plumbing Code recently mandated that PVC primer be color-coded, like the purple primer shown in the photo below. Color coding makes it easy for inspectors to see that a joint has been primed before it was solvent-welded. The cement you use should be labeled for use with PVC pipe. Plumbers' sandcloth or emery paper eases burrs and removes old cement.

Funnel dispenser puts an end to tangles

For an easy way to dispense rope, twine, yarn or string without tangles, take an ordinary funnel and fasten it to the wall. Set the spool in the funnel and thread the loose end through the narrow funnel opening. The rope or string will feed easily out of the funnel by pulling it. Now you'll be able to dispense and cut off only the amount you need, without having to untangle the spool first.

Lon Price
Indianapolis, Indiana

A good source for cheap glass

When you need glass to repair a broken window or need an odd-sized piece of glass for a new project that you're working on, try stopping at a local business that sells and installs replacement windows. Normally, these places have a pile of old windows on hand that have accumulated from other replacement jobs. There is usually little or no charge for the glass, since these businesses typically are happy to have you take it away.

Bryan Cunningham
Lancaster, Pennsylvania

GLASS TYPES, CHARACTERISTICS AND USES

Type	Characteristics	Uses
Sheet	Lowest cost, noticeable waviness due to thickness variations	General residential
Plate	Ground and polished much flatter than sheet glass	Large display windows and tabletops
Tempered	High impact strength and small, relatively harmless fragments when shattered	Patio doors, French doors, skylights, overhead windows and automobiles
Heat-absorbing	Absorbs heat and reduces building cooling loads; produced in various degrees and shades	Tinted glass, ovens, fireplaces and grills
Reflective/ Low-E	Metallic film reflects infrared waves, but not visible light; produces cooling effect in summer and heating effect in winter	Residential and commercial

No more stray spray tubes

I find it annoying when I need to use a spray lubricant, such as WD-40, and discover that the plastic tube for the spray nozzle is missing. This means that I have to hunt one down from another can. Here's a simple and handy remedy to keep from losing the spray tubes. I take an ink pen that has run dry (I've found that Bic-brand pens work the best) and remove the ink cartridge but keep the cap. I attach the pen body to the side of the spray can with masking or duct tape. Then I drop the spray tube into the pen body and replace the pen cap. Problem solved.

Timothy Hoffman
Middletown, Pennsylvania

Ice scraper trenches

When I install garden lighting, I've found that a metal ice scraper (the kind used to clear ice from walks and driveways) works well for digging narrow trenches to bury low-voltage wire. The ice scraper cuts a deep trench for the wire, which helps to minimize the possibility of accidentally damaging the wire with garden tools later on. Trenching with an ice scraper is easier than digging with a shovel, and best of all, you don't have to refill the trench with dirt when you're done. After the trench is cut, I lay the wire in place and use a cedar shingle to push the wire down into the crack (use a shingle rather than the scraper blade so you don't accidentally damage the wire). This method works especially well along walks, and the trenching process is nearly invisible.

Chuck Snyder
Hereford, Pennsylvania

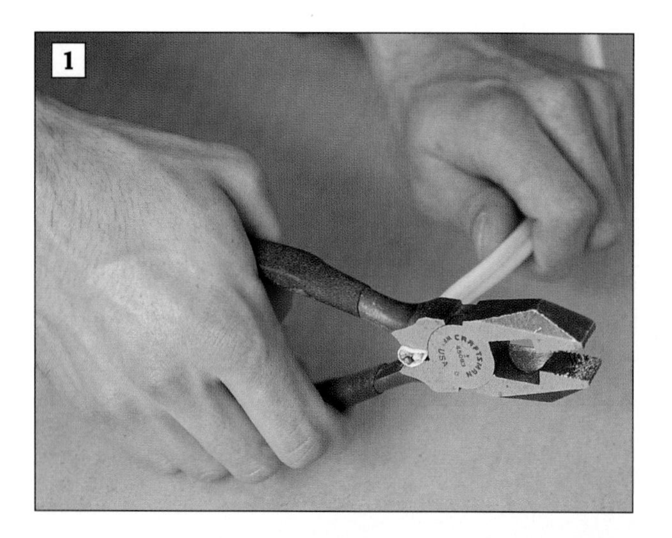

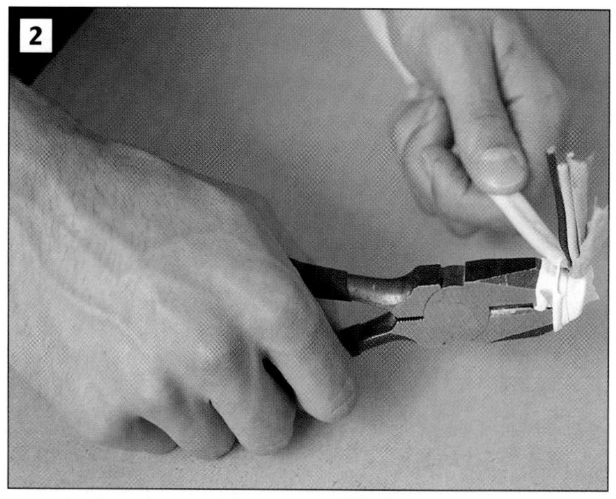

Stripping wire—just squeeze, peel and snip

To remove the sheathing from ROMEX-type wire cable without nicking the wires, I place the cable between the handles of a lineman's wire cutters and squeeze (See Photo 1). The pressure causes the outer sheathing to split. NOTE: This step works best if you squeeze the cable at several points around the end you're trying to split. It can then be peeled away by rolling the insulation back with the pliers (See Photo 2) and removed by snipping it off (See Photo 3). This method works best with 14-gauge or larger copper wire.

John Murphy
Cumberland, Maryland

Although actually a trade name, ROMEX is generally used to describe one class of flexible vinyl-sheathed cable. With the exception of the ground wire, which is sometimes left bare or covered with paper, each wire in a ROMEX cable is individually insulated. ROMEX cables come in three types for varying uses (See chart, right) and typically aren't run inside of conduit.

THREE TYPES OF ROMEX CABLE

Name	Use	Wire count	Makeup
NM	**Dry**	**2-3**	**Ground wire plastic wrapped**
NMC	**Dry**	**2-3**	**All wires in solid plastic**
UF	**Underground**	**2-3**	**All wires in solid, water-resistant plastic**

Parts for this wheelbarrow modification include an axle rod, two U-style bolts with washers and nuts, lock washers to hold the wheels on the axle and end caps to cover the ends of the axle. You can find these supplies at most hardware stores.

Three-wheel barrow takes a load off

Three years ago, my father had his hip removed. Because he was still active, and wanted to work around the house, he made a wheelbarrow that would still be operable without having to lift the handles to move it. He came up with this three-wheeled design by adding an axle and two wheels beneath the back legs of the wheelbarrow. It was a simple project that made use of parts that had been lying around his workshop and garage.

To modify your wheelbarrow, attach an axle beneath the legs of the wheelbarrow with U-style bolts (See photo, right). You may need to drill holes through the legs to attach the U-bolts. Then slide the wheels onto the axles and hold them in place with snap washers and axle caps. The larger the diameter of the wheels, the further up the wheelbarrow will tip and the easier it will be to roll over rough ground.

Dale A. Reilly
Tucson, Arizona

Member Projects

Completing a project is always a satisfying moment for the handyman. Stepping back and enjoying the fruits of all our hard work makes us forget the frustrations that can accompany many projects. And it makes us want to share our finished projects with others. In this section of *Members' DIY Secrets,* you'll find a gallery of clever and innovative projects accomplished by fellow Club Members, along with brief accounts explaining how and why these projects were done. As you review these pages, we hope you'll find the inspiration you need to complete another successful project of your own.

Furniture

"Sawdust" racks one up

When one of my daughters-in-law asked if I could build her a floor-standing quilt rack for displaying a quilt that her grandmother had made, I came up with this colonial design in time for her and my son's wedding. It was a hobby project that I worked on in my spare time. It really didn't take long—only parts of three days. Waiting for the finish to dry took the longest.

I improvised a little on the style of the quilt rack. Because it is an antique-looking piece, I decided to use pinned through-tenon joints to hold the uprights to the cross supports. No nails or metal fasteners were used.

The wooden pins look great and allow the rack to be easily taken apart for moving or storage. Although I chose to use pecan wood, any hardwood would have also worked.

My woodworking is more of a hobby than a business, but this quilt rack has been so popular that I've had to make several as gifts and have even sold a few!

Jesse "Sawdust" Stewart
Ponca City, Oklahoma

A grand-prize clock from father

My daughter was getting married and I wanted to make something special for her, so I decided to build a grandfather clock. Although I have worked with wood all my life (either with small woodworking projects or building projects), I had never attempted a fine-furniture building project before this one.

Since this was to be a special gift, I wanted it to be my own design rather than one from a kit, so I sat down and drew up plans. I had access to a supply of walnut wood from a tree that had been felled by an Alaskan mill about 15 years ago. I squared it up and planed it to size before I started to build, making small changes as I went along. The available wood meant that my only cost was for glass, hardware and clockworks.

We live in northern California and, due to the large amount of snow that we receive in the winter, I usually have a good deal of time off from my job driving a cement mixer. I used this time to build the clock in my garage workshop. Although it only took me two months to complete, and it was ready for my daughter's wedding, my wife and my friends convinced me to hold onto the clock until it was time for the county fair. I disagreed with them at first, but now I'm glad that they made me enter it. The clock won a blue ribbon in its class, and even won the "Best of Show" prize for all of the woodworking categories. This award made the clock eligible for entry into the state fair competition, but I didn't enter it there since my daughter had been very patient and didn't want to wait another year to see her wedding gift.

The most important lesson I learned from this project was never build something this big and fragile when you live in northern California and your daughter lives in Virginia—it was more expensive to ship the clock out east than it was to build it. Of course, it has all been worth it knowing the joy my wedding gift has brought to my daughter and son-in-law.

Ed Brack
Mt. Shasta, California

Not your typical homework

I made this 13-ft. oak cabinet while taking my 16th year of adult wood shop. I've made a number of projects through our local adult education program. It's a fun way to get to know people with similar interests. Not only do they provide all the necessary equipment, but the mess is made in somebody else's shop.

I use the shelves on top of the oak cabinet for showing off various knickknacks and photographs, while the bottom cabinets hold my stereo unit, as well as my Christmas dishes and decorations. I bought three pieces of marble to place on the tops of the lower cabinets. It makes a beautiful display surface. There are hidden light strips installed on the underside of six of the shelves so that my treasures are visible at night, too.

Florence Bogstad
Northridge, California

An island made of oak

When a neighbor of mine was relocating from central Texas to Arizona and didn't want to pay the transportation costs of moving his extra lumber (he had already moved it from Oregon to Texas), I gladly took the lumber off his hands. I used the lumber to build this butcher-block island for our kitchen. The top, legs and bottom shelf are all laminated oak. I designed a small drawer to store utensils, and installed a towel rack on the side opposite the drawer.

The island is assembled completely with screws so that it can be easily disassembled.

Editor's Note: To finish eating surfaces like butcher block, use linseed oil or salad bowl oil. Both are nontoxic when they dry and can be simply rubbed into the wood. Reapply the finish periodically for lasting protection.

J. C. Foster
Horseshoe Bay, Texas

Compact corner computer station

As my wife and I began using our home computer more and more, the old desk we had it on just wasn't cutting it. After shopping around and seeing the outrageous prices being charged for pressed-board computer desks, and the generic look of the desks within our price range, I decided to build my own. The desk I made measures 7 ft. long × 4 ft. wide. I used two sheets of white birch plywood, covering the work and shelf surfaces with black laminate. I finished the desk with four coats of hard, clear water-based finish. The whole unit can be broken down into six major parts: two desk surfaces and the monitor shelf, a drawer unit, a file cabinet and the bookshelf.

I've loved woodworking since I was a kid helping my dad remodel houses. In junior high school, I couldn't wait until shop class. Now that I have my own small shop building in the backyard, I'm always looking for new woodworking products and techniques.

This desk has been my most challenging furniture project to date. Building it has enabled me to learn many new techniques, including working with laminate and veneer. Most of all it taught me patience, and I think it's paid off.

Dean Hallal
Sumter, South Carolina

Double-duty toy box

A few years ago, I discovered how much I enjoy woodworking when I built an entertainment center. For my daughter's second birthday, I wanted to give her a bookcase and toy box made by her father. I decided to build a combination unit with shelving and a toy box with a lid. I sketched a design and even tried out some new techniques while I worked. Building the project in my spare time, I was able to complete it in about a month's time.

The bookcase is 4 ft. tall, and the toy box is 2½ ft. wide by 3 ft. long. The back, sides and front are made from 10-in.-wide pieces of pine edge-glued and doweled together. The toy box lid is also glued and doweled and overhangs the toy box on two sides. It's attached with a 29-in. length of piano hinge. Special lid support hardware on each side of the lid help hold the lid open so that my daughter can look for her toys without my wife and me worrying about the lid coming down on her. I took special care to match the porcelain knob on the lid with the knobs on my daughter's daybed. This was an enjoyable project for me and keeps my daughter busy with her toys. It was really nice to give her a beautiful piece of furniture made by her daddy.

Rick Prall
Mt. Juliet, Tennessee

Grandpa on cradle detail

This cradle project came about in part from my wife's "honey-do" list. We have two young grandchildren, so my wife suggested that I build them a cradle. I sized the proportions of the cradle so that it would fit an appropriate-sized cradle mattress. The wood I selected was cherry and the design is simple (I had to rush things because the third grandchild was on the way). I'm particularly proud of the detailing on the inside face of either end (See center photos). Here's how I did it. I do not like decals, nor could I draw these animal shapes easily, so I bought a pantograph. Using a router with a 60° chamfering bit and an old coloring book, I practiced on some scrap lumber and became pretty good at duplicating patterns in wood.

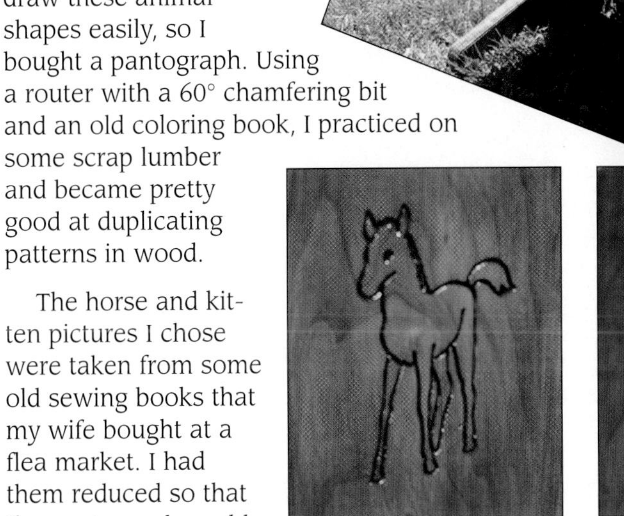

The horse and kitten pictures I chose were taken from some old sewing books that my wife bought at a flea market. I had them reduced so that the pantograph could copy them at ⅔ their original size. Once I had routed the designs into the end panels, I taped off the edges of the designs and sprayed the routed lines with flat-black paint. When the paint dried, I peeled off the tape to reveal two clear animal shapes.

To make sure that the cradle rocks smoothly and quietly, I used ¼-in.-dia. plastic tubing to serve as bushings for the pivot bolts in the legs. I then counterbored the holes for bolt heads and nuts to keep sharp edges safely out of harm's way. I attached the cradle with ¼-in-dia. shoulder bolts that are long enough to pass through the thickness of the cradle legs and the arms from which the cradle swings. To finish the wood, I applied a non-toxic, high-gloss varnish. As luck would have it, I finished the cradle just in time for the birth of our third grandchild.

Dale McCune
Blairsville, Pennsylvania

Cabinet shows that it makes sense to customize

This entertainment center is based on a set of magazine plans that I modified in order to better fit our particular needs. This piece has differently styled doors than the original plans as well as a newly designed drawer. I also installed more shelves to increase the display space and functionality of the entertainment center. It took me about four weeks to complete the project, which is actually three cabinets joined together. The doors are made of solid red oak, while the balance of the cabinet is red oak plywood. It's just what we needed.

Hill W. Kulik
Apopka, Florida

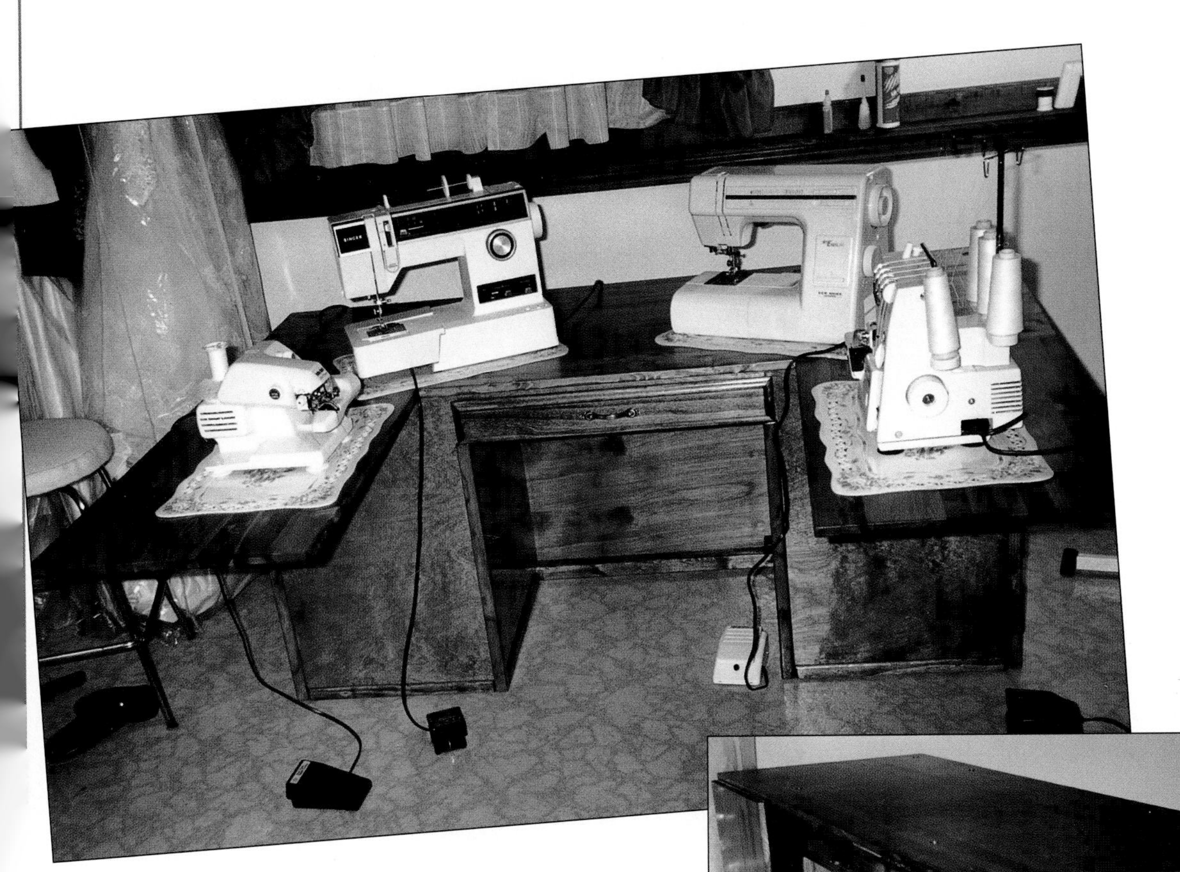

Sew much more room

I built this sewing station for my wife's various sewing machines and accessories. Since she couldn't find anything on the market that she liked, I decided to design and build the work center from scratch. I started with a 2 × 2 frame, which I then enclosed in plywood. I laminated the top from two sheets of plywood, applied edge banding and made hinged extension wings on both sides in order to accommodate all of my wife's sewing equipment. These drop-down wings provide much-needed space when they are fully extended but can also store conveniently flat against the sewing station for times when there's a little less work to be done. I put drawers on the sides rather than in the front so that they wouldn't interfere with the extension wings. My wife is pleased with her roomy sewing station and I'm happy with my first design of this kind.

Gary Link
Ft. Gratiot, Michigan

Gary's sewing station design includes hinged tabletop extension wings that fold conveniently out of the way when not in use. He installed drawers on the sides of the workstation rather than in front to keep them accessible when the extension wings are folded down.

Stand by your bed

When we purchased a new, taller mattress for our bed, the existing end tables became too short to be convenient. While looking through a surplus store, we found some 18-in.-sq., ¼-in.-thick polished marble slabs. Since we thought they would make ideal tabletops for our bedroom end tables, we bought four slabs.

I had some ¾-in.-thick oak boards just waiting to be used. I wanted to wrap the marble edges with oak and have this oak apron serve as the primary support for the tabletop weight. I rabbeted the oak aprons on both the top and bottom shelves so that the oak apron pieces would be flush with the top of the marble and support it from beneath.

I was concerned that a ¾-in.-thick leg may look flimsy, but I didn't want to combine two boards together into legs to square off the marble corners, so I notched the legs to receive the marble instead. This way, the legs actually make the marble look as though it is clipped at 45° at each corner, when in fact, it isn't.

The results of this project are two very attractive and functional end tables at just the right height for our new bed.

Gene Schell
Bartonville, Texas

Hard-working hutch

When my wife and I were newlyweds, our first apartment had virtually no cupboard space in the kitchen. We needed a place to store a variety of small kitchen appliances and glassware (most of which were all those new wedding gifts). My wife, Heidi, thought a hutch would be just the solution we needed, but we didn't have the money to buy one new.

At the time my tool collection was meager (circular saw, jig saw, drill and sander), but I promised her I'd give her hutch project a good try. Here's what resulted from my efforts. I built the carcase of the hutch from a single sheet of cabinet-grade birch plywood, so the outside would be defect free and flat. The doors are built from glued-up pine "handy panels," and the shelves, worksurface and hutch top are solid

pine boards. The back of the hutch is a sheet of 1/4-in.-thick pine plywood. I bought all of my hutch supplies from a local home center for less than $100.

I designed the hutch with a deep cabinet below and shelving above for two purposes: to store and hide those appliances and kitchen odds and ends we didn't want to see from day to day and to serve as our modest display case of finer glasses and pottery.

It's been seven years now since I built the hutch, and my woodworking skills and tool collection have grown. I'd like to build my wife a new and finer hutch using solid wood for the whole project, but she just won't part with this one—I guess she considers it to be my special wedding gift to her.

Grant Wilhelm
Indianapolis, Indiana

Finery finally finds a good home

Here's a corner display cabinet that I recently designed and built. I've made office chairs, hutches, dinette sets, entertainment centers, coffee tables, beds and vanities, but this project was my first attempt at building a three-sided display case. I built it so that we'd finally have a good place to store our family heirlooms and collectibles.

I built the upper and lower cabinets from oak and oak plywood and cut all the molding myself. I couldn't find the style of posts I wanted to use for the top of the display case, so I turned them on a lathe from solid oak. The glass upper case opens by way of a single door in front, and I used 1/4-in.-thick glass with polished edges to create sturdy shelves. The enclosed bottom of the cabinet also opens from a door in the front and has several shelves inside for other less attractive storables.

Editor's Note: Bryan mentions an important safety tip—when using 1/4-in.-thick glass for shelving, be sure to have the glass cutter polish the edges to eliminate the razor-sharp edges.

Bryan Yeckering
Owensboro, Kentucky

With a little help from my friend

I made this bed and nightstand for my 15-year-old granddaughter. She had seen similar pieces made by the grandfather of her best friend, and asked her dad if I could make one for her. I made everything by hand except the turned posts. The beaded panels for the bed and nightstand are pinewood and the rest of the parts are made of fir. It took about a month, working only six hours a week, to complete the two projects. Both my granddaughter and I are happy with the results. I wish to acknowledge the help of my neighbor, Don Marshall, whose handyman skills and knowledge contributed greatly to the success of these projects.

Wilbur C. Meier
Everett, Washington

Accessories

Rocking dory makes for smooth sailing

I built this rocking toy for friends living in Hawaii. The boat, modeled after a dory, was a gift to their son who was turning one year old. First birthdays are special celebrations for Hawaiians, so I wanted this toy to be just right. I crafted the hull from bent lauan plywood, which I then finished with paint and urethane varnish. Details like the boat's transom, seat, handle and gunwales are made from mahogany. For the rockers, I laminated two pieces of oak together and band-sawed the ends to simulate waves. I purposely selected oak that had knots in it, so the rocker arcs could follow the curves of the wood grain. I used screws to fasten the rockers and cross supports to the boat. Overall, the dimensions are 40 in. long, 20 in. wide and 16 in. high—perfect for the little skipper who is still "parting waves" with it today.

John Drigot
St. Paul, Minnesota

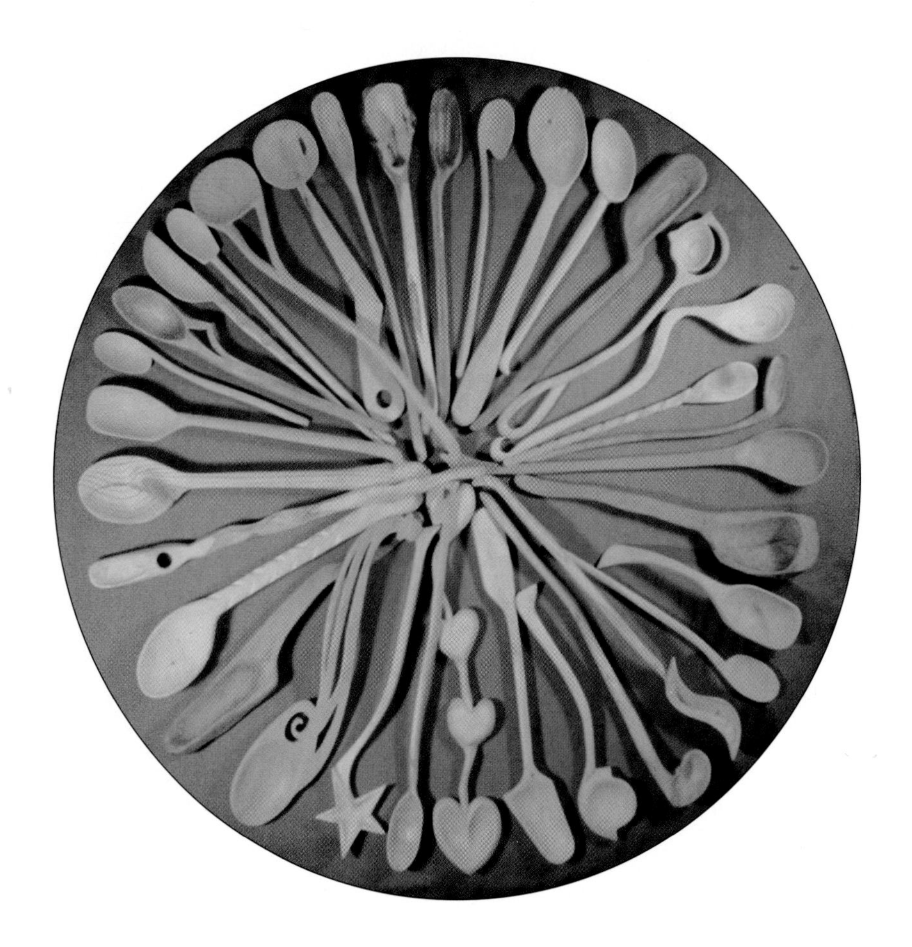

Member's collection gets the full scoop

Here is a sampling of some 75 spoons that I hand-carved in my spare time from wood that would have otherwise been scrapped or burned. The types of wood I used are numerous, varying from common woods like pine and oak to more unusual kinds like hickory and jelutong (a rubbery tree in the dogbane family). Each spoon has its own unique shape and detailing; I let the wood dictate the shape. Each spoon is fashioned from a single piece of wood. No two spoons are the same. Although I've had a few offers to purchase them, the spoons are not for sale. I just couldn't part with any of my hard work.

William Hichner
Tampa, Florida

Convertible wagon promises year-round fun

I made this convertible wagon/sled for my grandchild from recycled materials. The wood came from discarded pallets, and the wheels were salvaged from old lawn mowers. Since the rubber treads on the wheels were worn out, I "retreaded" them with my circular saw. I designed the wagon platform to be like a flatbed truck, with removable rails on all sides. The red canopy, which is an oak frame covered with a vinyl-coated fabric, is removable and part of the reason why I call the wagon a convertible.

I made the wagon handle by filling a one-gallon metal can with water, attaching a stovepipe to it and heating the water to boiling. I then inserted the oak handle in the stovepipe in order to steam it so that it could be bent over a curved template. The stainless-steel axles sit in V-grooves in the crosspieces at the bottom of the wagon and are attached with stainless-steel screws through holes in the axle shafts.

The biggest reason why this wagon is truly convertible is easy to see: I can remove the wheels so that plastic skis allow it to be used as a sled. The skis were made from 3/8-in.-thick plastic taken from an old office chair. These pieces were heated in an oven and bent into shape over a jig, then attached to wooden struts that fit onto the wagon's axles.

Jack Masucci
Ft. Lee, New Jersey

Sweating the details

This project is one of four miniature building structures I have built for collectors. I call it the "Old Country Store." The other three miniature buildings I've built resemble old-fashioned mansions. Although this store was tedious to build at times, it was also fun to make. I especially enjoyed building the stairs, banisters, windows and shingles. The whole building, which includes three floors and two staircases, stands 36 in. high. It also has counters and back shelves. I even fashioned antique barrels that fit inside to make it seem more like an old country store.

Sidney Clifford
Litchfield, Minnesota

Featherweight fountain

My Spanish-style fountain project is a fun, lightweight, easy-to-make piece of enjoyable backyard art. It can be used either as a fountain or as a planter. The primary building materials I used include 3 ft. × 10 ft. × 6-in.-thick sheets of polystyrene and a few tubes of craft adhesive. I used a hot wire tool (made from PVC pipe and a toaster wire connected to a small transformer) to cut the sheet polystyrene. The heat is controlled by a dimmer switch. This cutting method produces smooth, "pill-free" edges in the polystyrene, as opposed to cutting with a conventional hand saw, which leaves ragged edges that crumble.

About 10 years ago I owned a large department store. At that time, I learned how to work with polystyrene as a sculpting material. After a friend gave me large sheets of polystyrene, I decided to make this fountain. I visited a Miami historical site where I found the fountain I wanted to duplicate. Although my fountain is constructed completely from polystyrene, it looks and feels just like real stone. It is also easy to move once the water is drained.

I shaped pieces of the sculpture to the desired size, then assembled the fountain. After allowing the glue to dry, I determined how I wanted the water to flow and bored the necessary holes for the hoses that would supply water to the pump. Then, using equal parts concrete sealer and water, I sealed the area around the hose holes.

I added decorative elements to the fountain with a cake decorating bag filled with cement. I applied my desired design before painting and then allowed everything to completely dry. The final step was to paint the entire sculpture with two coats of fast-drying marine paint. After filling it with water, I installed my fountain pump, turned it on and have enjoyed the results ever since. The project took about a day to build and cost me around $90.

Ric Testani
Fort Lauderdale, Florida

A rising wall of wine

My inspiration to build this wine rack came from a similar design I saw once in a restaurant. I liked the way it displayed the bottles, which seem to defy gravity. After trying to find one to purchase without success, I finally decided to make one myself. It took me about a day to make from a single piece of 1 × 4 alder. Each hole is made with a 1¼-in. hole saw bit and drilled at a 20° angle in alternating directions. This way, each bottle rests at a 90° angle to the board, which keeps the corks moist and the wine fresh.

I mounted the rack to the wall using metal L-brackets and screws at both the top and the bottom. Now this vertical wine storage system gives me a convenient place to store my wine without taking up any cupboard space in my dining room. It also makes an unusual conversation piece.

John Kelsey
Pasadena, California

Mini mechanic's creeper makes toy tune-ups easy

Like many other Handyman Club Members out there, I've got a little handyman of my own coming through the ranks at home. My two-year old son Floyd thinks that he has to do everything that Daddy does, and of course, I encourage it. Last Christmas I got him a toy workbench, along with all the hand and power tools that were offered. But that still wasn't enough for my son. He liked Daddy's mechanic's creeper, so I set out to make him one of his own.

I constructed this simple creeper project using materials left over in my shop from other projects. It only took me two or three hours to build. I made the body of the creeper from ¾-in.-thick solid-core plywood and ran a ¼-in. "lip" lengthwise along both edges of the top side to match those on my full-size creeper. The headrest is made from an old shirt with alligators on it that my little helper had outgrown. Now, his favorite shirt lives on. I screwed a swiveling caster to each bottom corner of the creeper so that it would roll smoothly.

While building the creeper, I found that it's a good idea to place a drop of two-part epoxy on all four corners of each caster before screwing it in place. This adds a little more insurance in case your helper is as rough-and-tumble as mine. For an added touch, I varnished Floyd's creeper and put my Handyman Club of America sticker in the center of it. As you can see, my little helper loves it!

Paul Kuenzli
Bucyrus, Ohio

Intarsia eagle scene

My eagle scene is an example of an art form called *intarsia.* Intarsia was famous in the 12th century and was found mainly in Italy but is having a lively revival now in the United States. The term *intarsia* means to create pictures using different types and shades of thick wood. This technique is different from *marquetry,* which uses thin veneers.

The eagle scene was a commissioned work for a doctor and his wife who were former students of mine. The theme and topic were left totally up to me. Although it is an original design, I was influenced by other pictures of eagles in flight. It features natural colored woods from all over the world. I used no colored stain or paint—just a clear semi-gloss lacquer to preserve the wood and enhance the colors. It took me about 50 hours to build the 24-in.-dia. piece. I use a scroll saw for all of my intarsia cutting, as well as a 4½-in. belt sander. I put the final touches on it with a palm sander.

This particular form of art is taking off so well that I've been commissioned to make two 7-ft.-tall figures of Christ for two new churches, and now I'm doing a 10 × 10-ft. figure of Christ with Mexican-style art in the background for another local church.

Sister Shirley Wagner
Medford, Wisconsin

EAGLE PROJECT WOOD TYPES

Type	Part
Aspen	Tail, head
Walnut	Feathers, deer and water
Osage orange	Eye, beak
African ebony	Pupil of the eye
Oak and walnut	Claws
Padauk	Sunset
Maple burl	Snow-covered mountain
Cherry	Part of the rim
Oak plywood	Background

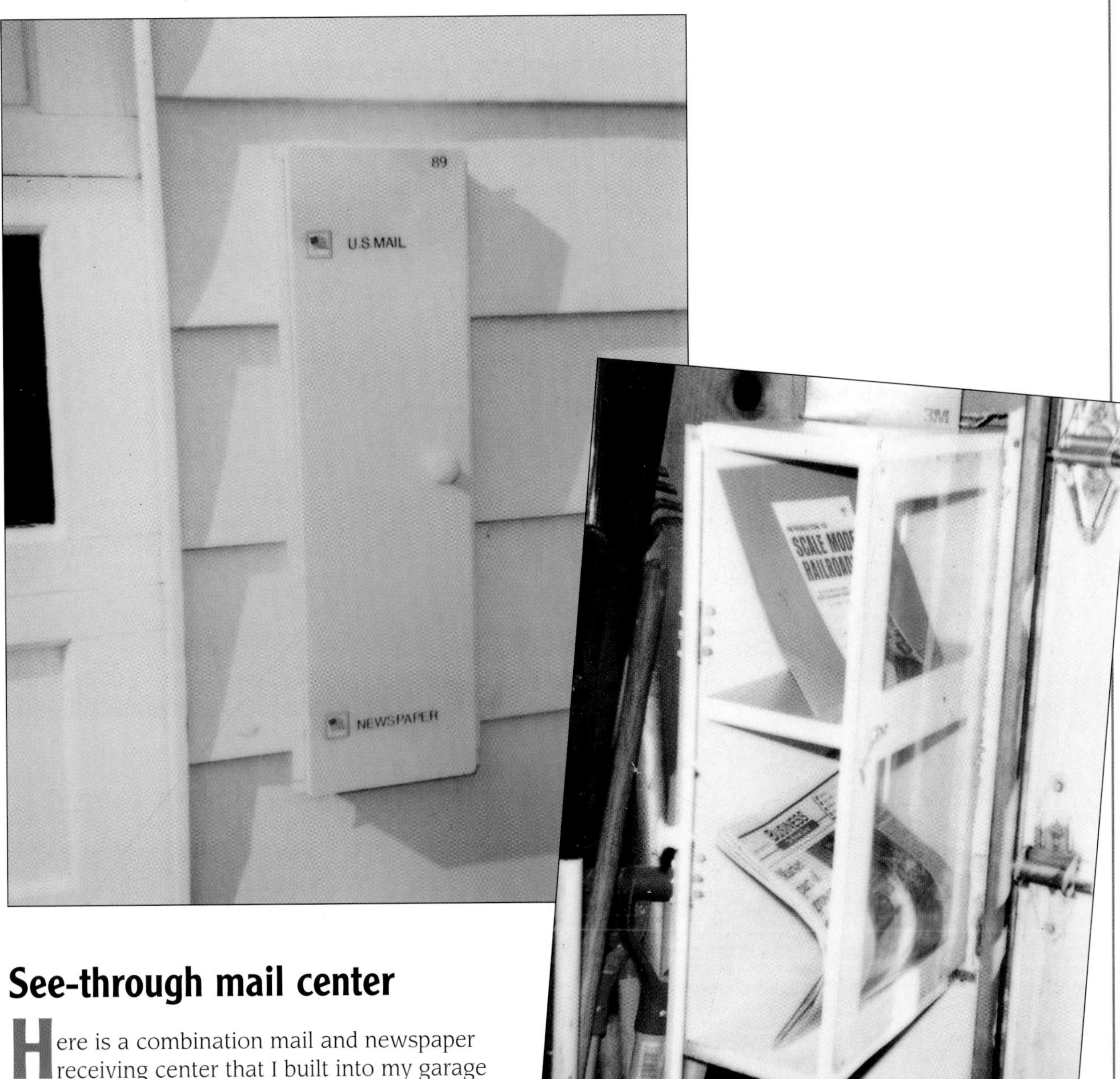

See-through mail center

Here is a combination mail and newspaper receiving center that I built into my garage wall next to the garage door. I wanted a box that would allow me to access the mail and newspaper from inside the garage. To accomplish this, I fashioned the box's inner case and shelves from wood and built a single large wooden door on the outside. I covered the side and back of the box with clear plastic panels. The back panel swings open on two hinges and is held shut with a latch hook. I decided to use the clear plastic so that I could see the contents of the box from across the garage. I assembled the box as a single unit, which I then slipped and fastened into a hole I cut through the wall and siding of the garage. It keeps my mail organized, visible and out of the way.

John Jones
Bristol, Connecticut

The horse that Grandpa tamed

I built this rocking horse for my two-year-old grandson. Although I used plans that I sent away for, I made a few changes for the sake of safety, comfort and appearance. Now, the piece has my personal touch. My first modification was to make the horse 2 in. wider. This gave it better stability and ensured that it wouldn't tip over while my grandson was riding it. I added a foam-cushioned leather seat in place of the hard, uncomfortable wooden one. I used an old purse strap for the halter and reins, which I decorated with upholstery tacks. The rocking horse is made entirely out of pine and is finished with three coats of clear acrylic polyurethane. I put many hours of hard work into this project, but watching my grandson rocking on it to his heart's content made it all worthwhile.

Horace Pereira
Cumberland, Rhode Island

Heirloom display box

I built this display box for my son and gave it to him on his 25th birthday. All of the items inside the box are family heirlooms. The knife is a 1940 Case XX four-blade bow back jackknife with a bone handle. It once belonged to my son's great-grandfather. The pistol is an 1896 Owl Head with a breakdown barrel to load and eject shells. It belonged to my father-in-law. The 1936 chauffeur badge was also his, when he drove a truck. I also included a 1955 Caterpillar belt buckle, which my father wore until he passed away.

When my son was born in 1968, he was the first male child born in the family in 20 years. At that time, my father-in-law said that the knife and the pistol were to go to my son, once he was old enough. When my father-in-law passed away in 1973, I built the box for the heirlooms. It took me a while to decide what type of box should hold these family treasures, but I finally decided on a design that I got from one of my wife's jewelry boxes. It is made of red cedar with dowel-pinned and glued joints. The inside is formed from polystyrene, which I contoured to fit each heirloom and then covered with velvet. The project took me about a day to build. Like other things I've made, I did not hurry. I have built a lot of projects, but I'm most proud of this one because of what it represents to my family.

Charles Stevens
Worthington, Kentucky

Backyard

Ambitious fencebuilding

I decided to construct a fence around my property for the sake of my pet German shepherd, my privacy and my serenity. In one week and with plenty of sunshine, I built 155 ft. of 6-ft.-tall fencing. It is custom-designed with two sets of large gates so I can drive in and store a travel trailer during the winter. I'm 52 years old, and I had just had knee replacement surgery before building the fence, so building the fence was quite an undertaking.

I dug all the post holes, poured my own concrete footings, set and leveled the posts, hung the 2 × 4 rails and screwed in more than 200 fence boards. The whole fence is made of cedar. I also hand-built my own lattice from strips of lath. Then I stained the fence driftwood gray.

I built a smaller version of the fence using leftover lumber to surround my flower garden along the house. Surplus concrete from other projects helped me create a water fountain next to the fence. I've planted flowers to help conceal the concrete.

Since I own only basic tools, I built the fence with a circular saw, shovel and drill. I'm very proud of the results.

Joyce Verhaag
Spokane, Washington

Club Note

Joyce's fence project proves that you don't need an elaborate set of tools to produce great-looking projects. The secret to successful project results are careful project planning, a working familiarity with the tools you use and patience.

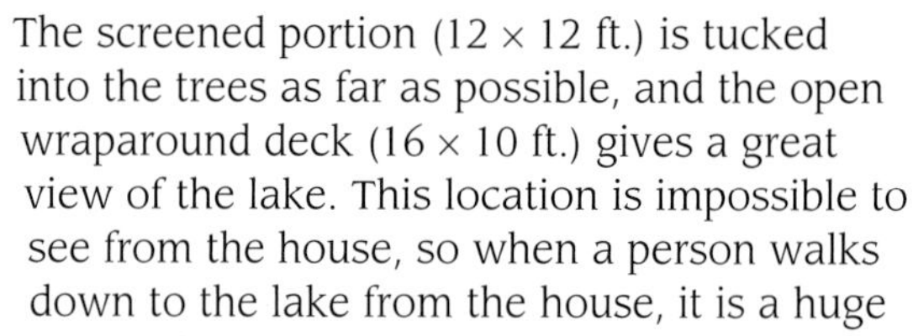

Lakeside getaway

My house is set back more than 300 ft. from the lakeshore, so it receives no cooling breeze from the lake. It is impossible to enjoy the lake or even see much of it from the house. Until recently, we had no place to sit down by the lake, so we wound up sitting on our pontoon boat whenever we wanted to relax and enjoy the beach. For all these reasons, not the least of which being sharing our summers with the "Minnesota state bird"—the mosquito—we thought it necessary to build a screened-in porch.

I'm a Frank Lloyd Wright fan, so the run-off stream at the east side of our lake property provided the perfect location to construct my own "Falling Waters" deck and screenhouse. I decided to construct the screen porch to span the stream. The screened portion (12 × 12 ft.) is tucked into the trees as far as possible, and the open wraparound deck (16 × 10 ft.) gives a great view of the lake. This location is impossible to see from the house, so when a person walks down to the lake from the house, it is a huge surprise. The entire project is set at a 45° angle to the lake, so that two sides of the porch face the water instead of just one.

I am truly a weekend warrior and not a professional. I started the project in May and completed it in August. In order to be confident about the strength of the structure, I used lumber one size up from what was required by building code. Doing this has also eliminated any shake or bounce on the deck. To keep costs down I used treated lumber, waited a year, and then had a semi-transparent stain custom-mixed to match some nearby tree bark. My intent was to make the project less visible from the lake. I used landscape fabric under the decking of the screened porch for bug control, and all of the soffits are screened as well. Since we're in a bit of a tornado belt, I used hurricane strips to connect the rafters to the headers of the roof, which has already paid off.

When the stream is flowing it's possible to hear several small waterfalls. I've also installed a 55-GPM pump that recirculates water to and from the lake during dry periods. The inside of the porch is done in a seaside theme complete with a "sand bar" refreshment area (See photo, right). The bar top was first filled with beach sand, clam shells and other things from the sea, then filled with a clear epoxy that is quite durable. This bar is a real conversation piece. I installed indirect lighting below all of the railings to give the deck a glow in the evening. A large ceiling fan cools the screen porch on hot, still nights.

I worked from a set of plans I drew up for the deck and porch, taking into consideration those needs the project had to fill: view, bugs, cost, visibility and entertainment value. The final project has fulfilled those needs, in addition to many others. I'm very pleased with the results.

Todd Bendtschneider
Howard Lake, Minnesota

Food court is for the birds

For all you avid bird watchers out there, here's a simple structure you can build to attract a host of bird species. My bird food court is composed of a simple wooden roof structure at a 45° pitch built from 2 × 4s and covered with exterior-grade plywood and shingles. The roof is supported by 4 × 4 pressure-treated posts, with a pipe running across the posts to hold up all of my bird feeders. The sheltered design keeps the birdseed dry.

I went to our nearest home improvement center and bought all of the necessary materials to build it. My husband, Bruce, built it according to what I had in mind for our backyard.

An added bonus of the project happens in late spring, when the area around the feeders becomes a whole circle of sunflowers that grow from fallen seed. It's beautiful. I love watching the flowers bloom in the backyard, and the birds love it even more.

Rose and Bruce Harned
Southington, Ohio

Gotta get a glider

I made these gliders for my kids. They have a large back porch and yard but no place to sit and enjoy those warm summer evenings. I purchased some plans, made some modifications to the designs and built the two gliders you see here. The plans I built from called for cedar, but no one around here carries it, so I made these gliders from good, white pine. You could also use treated lumber, if you wanted to—or any other wood that stands up to the elements outdoors. After I used my sander to smooth all the ends and sides, I used redwood mahogany stain to get the red finish I was looking for. The next day, I applied a clear, gloss spar varnish topcoat.

My children have found good use for these projects, and neither bench took me more than a day to build.

Frederick Klaas
Kimball, Michigan

Gazebo has family waiting in line to relax

My husband, Bob, designed and built this unique corner gazebo in our backyard. The gazebo, which was built with redwood, has a shake shingle roof. Bob had particular fun hanging onto the roof so as to not fall while he was shingling it. The inside ceiling is lined with cedar strips, which not only look great, but smell great, too. Bob also attached a fan to the center of the ceiling, which was a little tricky because of the pitch. The fan looks and works great, especially on those hot summer days in Arizona.

Bob also installed fluorescent lights around the outer edge of the gazebo. These fixtures light both the inside and outside, providing a pleasant place to sit at night. To give us the final relaxing touch, he hung a set of speakers running off of our radio and CD player in the house. Now we can enjoy our favorite music in the backyard.

We all just love this gazebo—our daughters, grandkids, family and friends. Sometimes you even have to wait to get an open chair. Bob has given us a great place to enjoy the outdoors, right here at home. I'm a very proud wife.

Ellen and Bob Frisby
Glendale, Arizona

Arbor goes up better with teamwork

This arbor makes an attractive entrance to our rear deck. My husband and I saw a smaller version of the arbor while we were on a walk one day, and we thought it would make a good trellis for our fast-growing trumpet vine.

We used 4 × 4 posts and two 1 × 8s with half moons cut from their centers to make the archway. I enjoy the oriental appearance of this feature. We decided to use vinyl lattice since our cold, wet winters, along with the ground heaving up, can be terribly hard on wood lattice. The color we chose for the lattice contrasts nicely to the cherry stain that was used on the pine wood. The 4 × 4s are lag bolted to the deck rails for extra support.

My husband and I completed the entire arbor in a weekend for under $100. I've always enjoyed working on outdoor projects, and it seems that the more I do, the more my husband, Ken, is beginning to enjoy getting involved, too.

Joy and Ken Mott
Sandpoint, Idaho

A deck with a view

I decided to build a deck as a way to enjoy the natural beauty of the Hudson River valley that runs behind our house. It's a great place to watch jets flying out of Stewart Air Force Base, as well as fireworks over the river. Nestled in the woods just to the west and below us is a park with baseball fields, where games take place on spring and summer evenings, and where hot air balloons land when the hot air balloon festivals are going on. There's also the beauty of autumn, when the trees change colors.

Before we built this deck, we had to run outside and stand at the bottom of our driveway to enjoy all of the outdoor things I've mentioned. Also, with four children (two of them being teens) living in a 1600-sq.-ft. house, we were a little cramped for space, so we thought a deck would give our home more living space.

After helping some friends with their decks (on a smaller scale), I started to formulate my own deck plans, taking into consideration that I wanted the deck to be usable even on days when the weather isn't cooperating. I decided to build it along the full length of the house so that we could throw parties and accommodate 20-30 people on the deck comfortably.

The larger, 56-ft. deck also suits aesthetic purposes. I planned on an open area for sunning and outdoor parties as well as an area protected overhead in case of inclement weather. This part also provides shade when the sun gets too hot. We can bring the plants here too, when we have to get them out of the rain or the sun.

After I checked with the city and obtained a building permit, I began the project around

In order to begin construction on their new deck, the Kings had to first tear off an existing enclosed second-floor porch.

The old porch door would provide access into the Kings' new covered porch on the right-hand side of the deck.

Labor Day. We needed to tear off an existing second-floor porch first before the new deck construction could begin. Working odd hours, here and there and on weekends, we finished in early October, just in time for the fall colors. Although the photos don't show it, I eventually enclosed the whole area under the deck with latticework. I landscaped the entire yard the next spring and found that the area under the protected overhang is an excellent place for storage.

Since the deck has been finished, we have enjoyed many carefree days and nights outside. My only regret is that I didn't build it sooner.

George King
Fort Wayne, Indiana

As the deck nears completion, final details are added like stair and deck balusters and railings. Notice how the old porch has now been transformed into a more open, airy design.

Tiered waterfall solves shady problem

We used to have a dead area in our front yard that I could never successfully grow anything in. It is heavily shaded by large maples, which kept light away from new plants. I decided to give up the fight and fill the bare corner with a waterfall project.

My husband and I made three lily pad-shaped pools from ready-mix cement. To do this, we molded forms in a sand pile and then poured cement into them. We let them cure for one week and then water-proofed them with concrete water-proofing sealer. We positioned them so that the largest pad with two spouts sits over the two smaller pads. This way, water trickles down three tiers and into the recycle pond we built into the base. We also installed a small pond pump to circulate the water.

Now the sound of the falling water can be very soothing while I'm sitting or working outside. I put a variety of artificial plants around the pond to add some green foliage and color. Ken helped wire in several spotlights so that we could enjoy the lily pond at night. We have received many compliments from passers-by, but the best part was being able to work on this project together.

Joy and Ken Mott
Sandpoint, Idaho

Club Note

Most building codes require that outdoor electrical receptacles be ground-fault protected with GFCI outlets enclosed in watertight receptacle boxes. If your outdoor project requires electricity, like the Motts' waterfall does, check your local building codes before you install the wiring.

The bigger the better

In spring 1996, my wife and I decided to build a bigger garage. The plans that I drew up were for the biggest garage allowable by our city's building codes. I even had to get my neighbors' approval on the project. While it was under construction, the city inspector would drive through the ally every now and then to see how I was doing on the largest garage in town.

The garage stands 18 ft., 6 in. to the peak. It measures 32 ft. long by 24 ft. wide. It is both heated and insulated. I used 106 sheets of plywood, inside and out, to complete the garage. The structure took me two years to build, working well into the evenings after work.

I also built a new, spacious workshop in the loft of my garage. As a special storage feature, I cut three hinged doors in the top of my 19-ft.-long workbench to keep supplies all out of sight and the benchtop clutter-free. Now, the workbench can hold many more tools, nails and screws. I've labeled each hinged compartment to make sure that nothing gets misplaced and I can find things at a glance.

I had a lot of fun building my new garage and workshop. I'm looking forward to starting my new woodworking hobby, now that I have plenty of room to do it in.

Michael F. Yehle
LaCrosse, Wisconsin

Deluxe swing and pond

Here are two of my favorite backyard building projects—a chair-style swing and corner pond—that have been particular favorites of our guests. Both projects have given us many years of enjoyment.

The swing design is comfortable, particularly if you raise your arms and rest them on the chain spreader bar above the seat. Cushions also enhance the comfort of the swing, though I removed them here for clarity. Although I used nails to join the boards, you could also use screws. My swing could be built out of any weather-resistant wood such as white oak, teak, redwood or even treated lumber. I used cedar. The chains and hardware needed to hang the swing could vary but should not be skimpy. I used S-hooks where the chains meet to make taking the swing down easy.

The pond project design is really two tiered ponds with a waterfall flowing between them. The lower pool features a small fountain and a pump to circulate water back up to the upper pool. I carefully laid a fieldstone border around the entire structure and added plenty of plants to give the pond a more natural appearance. It's great to relax in our swing and hear the sound of falling water in our backyard.

Gene P. Schell
Bartonville, Texas

Screen porch conversion

My family used to enjoy spending time in a backyard screen enclosure that had a canvas roof, but we could only use it during warm summer months. I decided to put my handyman skills to work and make a more year-round screen house. I dismantled the old screen house and designed and built a wood-framed structure that uses the aluminum screened panels and screen door from the old patio enclosure (you can see them stacked against our garage in the photo at right). Originally I intended to throw the panels away, but I decided to use them on my new screen porch project. The combination storm window and screen panels give us the ventilation we need to cool our backyard "cabana" in the summer but can be closed to hold in the warmth of sunlight in the winter.

I decided to make the porch framework as sturdy as possible, so I used 4 × 4s and pressure-treated 2 × 8s. There is only one door in the cabana. All of the other screen panels are attached to the 4 × 4 posts with screws. This was my first attempt at such a project, and I'm very pleased with the way it turned out. It only took my son and me three days to finish it, and we took our time to get the design just right. Our cabana gives us a place to enjoy our backyard, no matter what season it is.

Joseph A. Slicius
Brockton, Massachusetts

Second-generation deck

My original deck was 26 years old and needed to be replaced. It was a plain, 10 × 12-ft. structure with basic horizontal railing. I found it small, especially when I put a 60-in. round table with benches on it. I decided to build myself a larger, 11 × 14-ft. deck that had built-in benches on two of the three sides.

After seeing how easy it was to pull the old deck off—it was only spliced to the house—I decided to fasten the ledger board of my new deck to the house sill plate and header joist using 6-in. lag screws in pairs, spaced every 16 in. The old deck used 2 × 6s for the decking and 2 × 8s for the joists. Since these boards lasted 26 years, I decided to use the same size pressure-treated lumber for my new deck. I got the lumber from a local, independent lumberyard that sells better quality lumber than the wholesaler in the area. I was able to reuse the old cement footings so I didn't have to pour new ones.

One special feature of the deck is the benches. I found that straight-back benches built at 90° were not very comfortable, so I designed a bench seat with a slant back that extends all the way to the deck boards. Everyone who sits on them finds this design more comfortable. Once the horizontal rails were in place, I added 2 × 2 vertical rails for safety. This way, kids will not be able to fall off the deck.

The project was fun to do along with my 27-year-old son. Together, it only took us six days over the July 4 weekend. Relaxing has never been easier.

John Holmstrom
Stamford, Connecticut

The "Grandpa Express" is right on time

This train engine backyard toy was requested by my daughter-in-law, who had seen a similar project at a pumpkin farm. She asked if I could make one for my two grandsons. No problem. I used a 55-gallon plastic drum for the engine's main body. You could use a steel drum of the same size, but I decided on plastic because if the kids fell against it, they wouldn't get hurt. Plastic is also lighter and easier to move, yet it is strong enough to support both of the boys if they climb on it.

The cradles under the barrel are 2 × 6s, and I used ¾-in.-thick plywood for both the body and the wheels. I made the cab floor support with a 2 × 4, and I slotted and bent a ½-in.-thick piece of plywood for the roof. Inside the cab, I mounted hot and cold bathroom faucet handles to act as controls so that the kids can pretend they're actually driving the train. I hung a small cowbell on top of the barrel and ran a string into the cab with a wine cork at the end, which can be pulled to ring the bell.

Due to the time it took the paint to dry, the project took approximately one week to complete. However, all the pieces can be cut and assembled in about a day and a half. The best part of the project was delivering it to my grandsons' house and seeing the look of delight in their eyes. Now, the toy engine sits in their backyard and is used heavily by all the kids in the neighborhood.

David T. Hughs
Livermore, California

Remodeling

Kitchen of the sea

My husband, James, and I built these beadboard yellow pine kitchen cabinets at our shop at home, then installed them in our cabin on the San Juan Islands. During the renovation of the rest of the kitchen, we tried to include as many things from the beach as we could. The backsplash below the cabinets is made from rocks that we hand picked off the sand. There's a crab claw next to the faucet handle, and an oyster shell to hold the soap. We even fastened driftwood logs at the corners of the lower cabinets. By incorporating all of these sea items into our remodeling project, we wanted to create a certain beach feeling, even while we sit inside the cabin on rainy days.

James and Marlene Parker
Seattle, Washington

Sunroom and shop to boot—all it takes is compromise

We have a great backyard that borders on a park. However, it also sits on a flood plain that the mosquitoes just love. We needed a way to enjoy the outdoors without being bothered by the bugs. My wife had been talking about a sun porch for years, so we compromised—she could get her sun porch if I could extend out the front of the garage for my workshop. This is the remodeling project that resulted.

When I pulled down the old steel soffit from beneath our second-floor walkout deck, I discovered a steel beam that ran the entire length of the structure. I sand-blasted off the rust, primed it, wrapped it in pressure-treated 2 × 4s and tied the rafters of the new porch into it. I did the same thing to the two vertical pipe columns that support the deck above the sunroom to conceal them. All the framing lumber and electrical fixtures were salvaged from a department store remodeling job. The paneling I used to line the inside ceiling of the porch came from a school in our area.

Certainly the most unique aspect of the addition is the post and beam extension on the right side of the sun porch that juts out from the second floor. This support was used for a well that was drilled for the sprinkler system, long before we bought the house. We kept it as a tribute to both Frank Lloyd Wright and our own eclecticism. It makes for a very good conversation starter.

David Fassett
Elkhart, Indiana

As this photo taken before the remodeling project shows, the new sunroom would start at the front edge of the second-floor deck and extend out into the yard. David saw this as a good opportunity to add on to the front of his garage at the same time for a workshop.

Here the sunroom and workshop framing nears completion and illustrates how David enclosed steel beams and posts by wrapping them with wood. All of the framing lumber you see here came from a department store remodeling project—a nice way to pare down the project budget and recycle at the same time.

As the project nears completion, David finishes the sun room ceiling with more recycled material—paneling from a local school. Notice the doorway at the far end leading to the new workshop.

Custom covers keep out critters

I am a full-time pest control operator in south Florida. Since we do not have cold winters, the problem with insects and rodents is a never-ending challenge. Besides failing to prevent pest entry, I've found that plastic vent covers also look terrible. To help prevent rodents and insects from entering through eave vents, and to make these vents more attractive, I've designed special covers to be used beneath wood soffits. I call them CHARDT covers.

CHARDT vents are designed to fit a standard 4-in.-wide vent opening, though any size opening could be outfitted by modifying my design. I built a plywood template jig to help me cut screening to 4 in. wide by 8 ft. long without measuring. I build each section of vent by fastening a layer of galvanized wire mesh and insect screening to fir framing members held directly in the jig. I put the wire mesh in front of the insect screening to protect the screening from being torn by the sharp claws and teeth of rodents, particularly squirrels.

My CHARDT covers keep eave vents insect- and rodent-free, and they look good, too.

Chris Chardt
Lake Worth, Florida

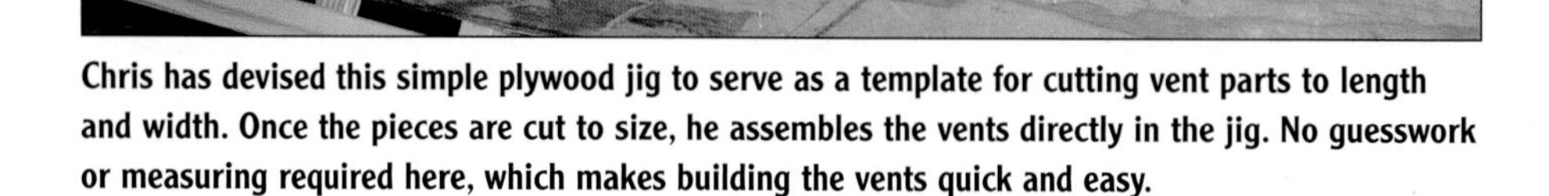

Chris has devised this simple plywood jig to serve as a template for cutting vent parts to length and width. Once the pieces are cut to size, he assembles the vents directly in the jig. No guesswork or measuring required here, which makes building the vents quick and easy.

Two-faced cabinet room divider

Before my parents bought their house, the previous owners added on an office that included a 6 × 10-ft. picture window that faced the living room. The window into the living room was useless, and we tended to cover it up with drapes and furniture anyway.

Recently, I decided to undertake some long overdue remodeling in the house office and drew up a plan that would make this wall more useful. I removed the old window and built a storage and display unit in its place out of oak stock and ¾-in.-thick oak plywood. I reframed the wall and designed the cabinet so that there would be shelves and cupboards facing both the office and living room. In effect, it's a cabinet with two faces. On the family room side of the unit, I made an area for a stereo, CD's and tapes and plenty of smaller and narrower shelves for pictures and collectibles (See photo, above). The office side contains a large bookcase, with plenty of storage space behind the lower doors. My cabinet sure beats a window with a bad view.

Ron Davidson
Cheney, Kansas

Ron's clever cabinetry turns a useless window space into a functional storage area for two separate rooms in the house. At the stage of construction shown here, you can still see from one room into another through the cabinet bottom compartments.

Not just any hole in the wall

Until recently, we had a bare, non-loadbearing wall between our kitchen and the dining room. We were also short of cabinet space in the kitchen. To solve this problem, and to liven up the interior of our home, I cut a 6 × 3-ft. hole in the wall and installed a pine sit-down breakfast bar and counter. Three children or two adults can sit comfortably at the bar. This opening also acts as a pass-through serving counter for the dining room. It is a much handier way to get the food from the kitchen to the table and really opens up the two rooms.

On the kitchen side, I built cabinets above the opening to the ceiling. Now we have considerably more storage space in the kitchen. The scalloped pieces below the cabinets were made from 1 × 8 pine boards. They conceal a 4-ft. fluorescent light that hangs above the counter, and also give our kitchen and dining rooms an added decorative touch.

Lance Kress
Hillsborough, North Carolina

At-home hideaway

This remodeling project began as a birch platform bed. Over the course of four weekends, my creativity got the best of me and I made a number of additions. I built a bookcase on each side of the bed, which also houses a TV and stereo components. To give the hideaway a gothic look, I sprayed two sections of large PVC pipe with stone finishing spray and installed them as faux "columns" on either side of the bed alcove. My wife eventually dressed the columns further with lace curtains and large burgundy pillows.

This room has now become our favorite room in the house. We spend many relaxing evenings reading, listening to music or watching TV on our convenient sofa bed. It has been a very popular project, and not just with us—everyone who comes over wants one built in their home, too.

Frank Verrichia
Sewell, New Jersey

Storage

Modular system packs 'em in

I am an average "weekend warrior" type handyman. I often justify the purchase of new tools with the money I am saving doing a job myself. Thus (like a lot of other Club Members, I'm sure), I have managed to accumulate quite a collection of "stuff" in my garage workshop.

As the "Before" picture reveals, my garage was a disorganized mess. This was mostly due to the fact that there was no specific place for anything. To solve my problem, I decided to create "storage modules" comprised of three main units, each of which holds particular kinds of shop equipment.

One cabinet houses all of my lawn and garden supplies, including a lawn mower, gasoline edger, string trimmer and a full complement of rakes, shovels, brooms and hedge trimmers. These items used to take up valuable garage space, especially during the seven months of the year when they weren't being used.

The middle cabinet houses all of my power tools. Included inside are a table saw, a wire-feed welder, all of my pneumatic tools and a host of hand tools. The bottom front of the unit can be pulled out and tipped upright to create a worktable with folding legs. The doors that conceal the power tools slide on a track. I also have incorporated a few drawers for miscellaneous other small items.

Like the power tool storage module, the workbench unit to the right of the center module has sliding shutters that reveal pegboard storage for hand tools. Power is controlled by a switch unit mounted into the face of the workbench, which services the overhead light, a built-in air compressor, a shop vacuum and a stereo.

What used to be a mess is now a source of pride for me. I'm sure that there are a lot of other handymen out there in a similar predicament to the one I was facing. Building storage units like these can be a great way to prevent a lot of the headaches. In addition to storing all of the equipment I own, the cabinets create enough room for two cars, four bicycles and a motorcycle in my modest two-car garage.

David Crittenden
Coppell, Texas

Hand-crafted toolbox catches eyes of carpenter's clients

Although I have a 600-sq.-ft. shop/garage, most of my handyman projects are done away from home. Being a self-employed carpenter who must take his tools with him to work, I had a storage problem when I bought a new truck some years ago. One possible solution was to buy either a plastic or aluminum box, which sells for $100-$250. Besides their relatively high cost, I couldn't find a toolbox that I liked.

I decided that the best remedy was designing and building my own toolbox out of wood. I made my box from local Florida cypress (a good weather-resistant wood) and attached the lids with stainless-steel piano hinges to keep them from corroding. I installed locks on both of the toolbox doors for added security. All of the screws are countersunk, and the screw holes are plugged with cypress wood plugs that I cut myself. The finish is marine polyurethane. Although this varnish was not cheap, it has been well worth the price as I have only had to refinish the toolbox once in 4½ years.

The whole project took me 30 hours to build and the final bill for materials came to about $60. The best part is the advertising that it provides. My homemade truck toolbox is better than any business card I could carry!

Kevin Kelly
St. Augustine, Florida

Shop organizing, bit by bit

In order to keep my various bits and drill accessories from being lost or damaged, I built this compact storage unit to keep them in. The cabinet hangs on the wall next to my drill press, which keeps all of the bits and accessories close at hand. Whenever I need to change bits, I know exactly where to go. There's no more rummaging through a junk drawer or messy toolbox to find what I need to finish a project!

When closed, the cabinet is 17 in. wide, 20 in. high and 7 in. deep. I made it from ½-in.-thick birch plywood and 1× pine. I chose these materials so that the drill bit unit would match the other woodworking stands and cabinets in my shop. As a special feature, the trays that hold the drill bits tip forward for easy selection. The shelves built into the door provide ample storage space for various accessories, such as sanding drums and countersink bits. This simple project has been a great way to organize my shop.

David Kirchner
Rapelje, Montana

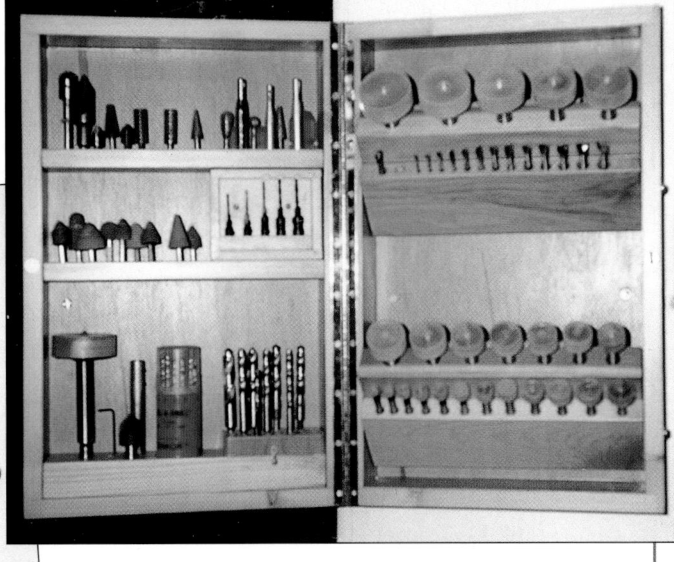

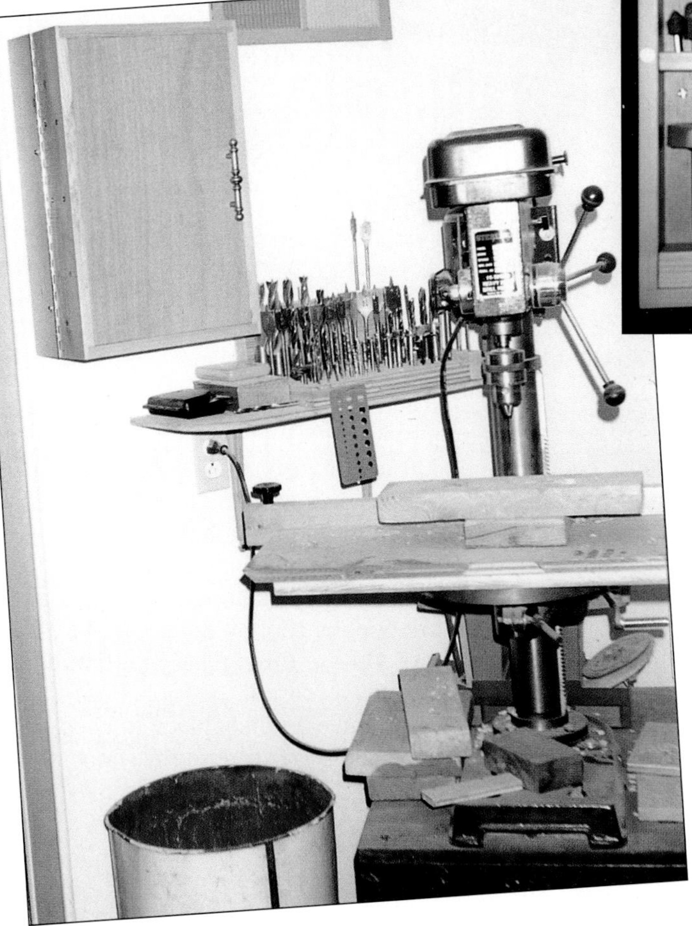

DRILL PRESS SPEEDS

Material	Hole dia.	Speed (rpm)
Plastic	1⁄16 in.	6000-6500
	¼ in.	3000-3500
	½ in.	500-1000
Soft metal	1⁄16 in.	6000-6500
	¼ in.	4500-5000
	½ in.	1500-2500
Steel	1⁄16 in.	5000-6500
	¼ in.	1500-2000
	½ in.	500-1000
Wood	1⁄16-½ in.	3000-4000
	½-1 in.	2000-3000
	1+ in.	700-2000

Note: Multi-spur bits, such as Forstner bits, should be used at low speeds (250-700 rpm)

Who loves tools? Ask Bryan.

I decided to build this chest to better organize my tools and keep them all in the same place. I included a number of special features in the design. There are four removable shelf caddies on each side of the cabinet that I use for storing drill bits, router bits and other accessories. To conserve space, I installed a tool tray that swings down from beneath the lower middle shelf. This tray holds my calipers and measuring tools. I store my yardstick and levels on hangers below the other two middle shelves. At the very top of the center tool chest, I built five removable trays. Each tray drops down by simply pinching two plastic tabs together.

The paint job on the front of the chest was all done by hand. It took four coats of paint and as many coats of gloss polyurethane to achieve the rich color and shiny finish I was hoping for. I chose to make the chest more interesting and appropriate for a workshop setting by painting a few of the more popular tool manufacturers across the doors. I chose these particular brand names because they represent the tools I use most often. Now, I have a handy place to keep them, and quite a storage fixture in my shop.

Bryan Yeckering
Owensboro, Kentucky

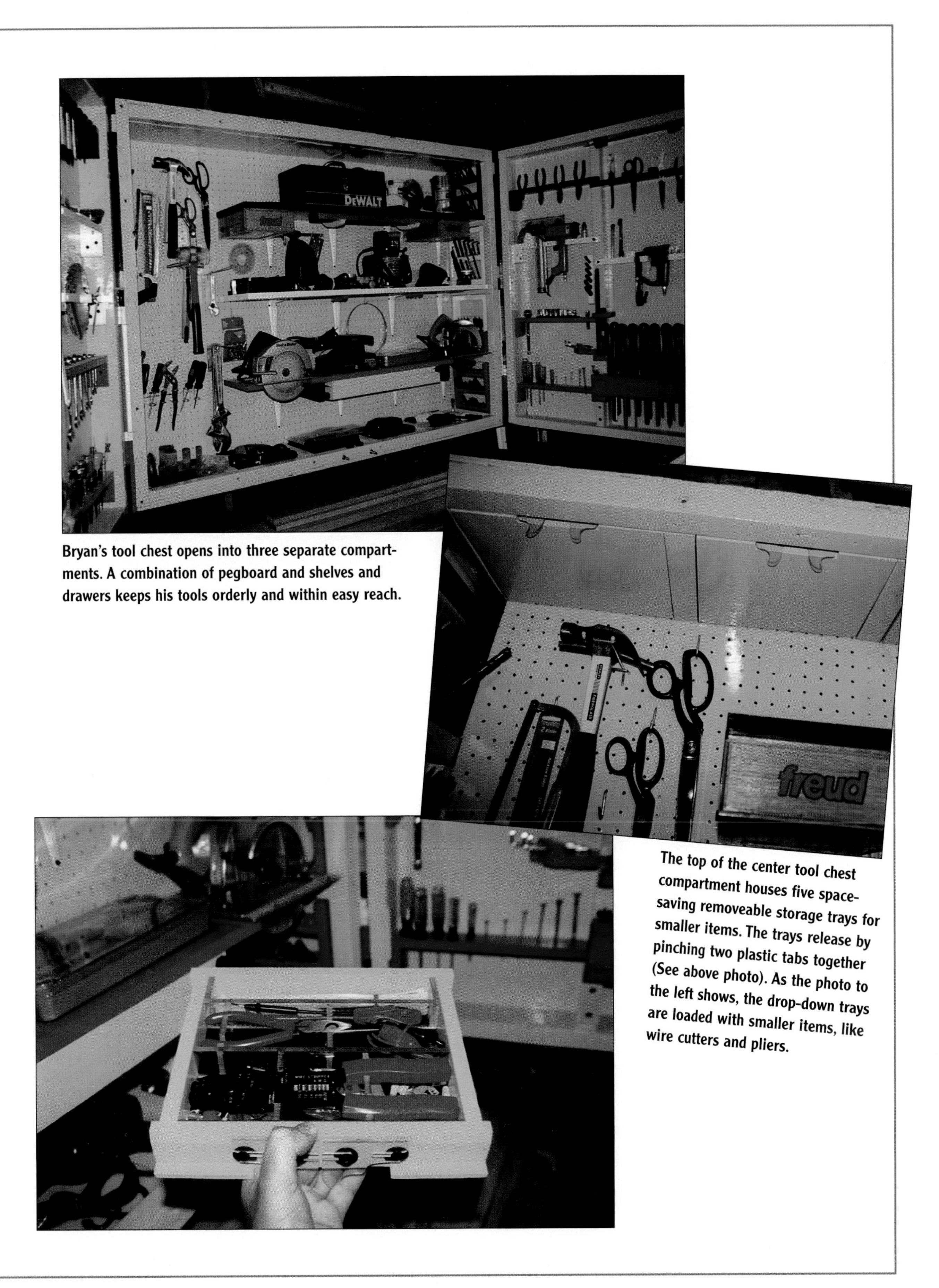

Bryan's tool chest opens into three separate compartments. A combination of pegboard and shelves and drawers keeps his tools orderly and within easy reach.

The top of the center tool chest compartment houses five space-saving removeable storage trays for smaller items. The trays release by pinching two plastic tabs together (See above photo). As the photo to the left shows, the drop-down trays are loaded with smaller items, like wire cutters and pliers.

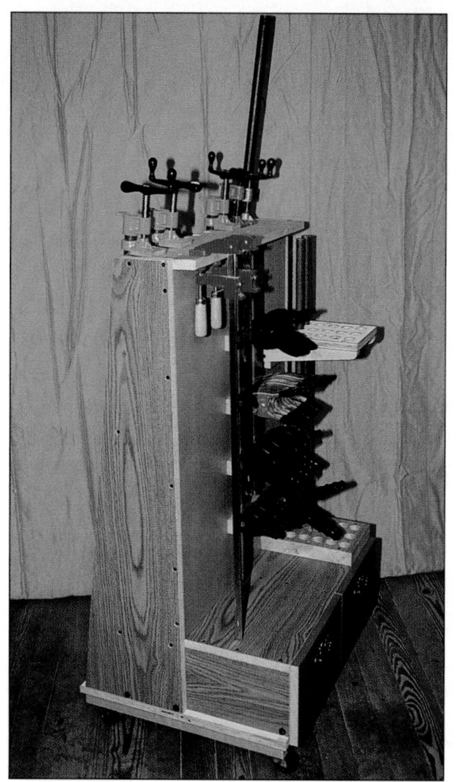

Clamping onto a good storage solution

My clamp rack is a convenient way for me to store all my shop wood clamps. As you can see in these photos, it stores a number of clamps neatly and in a very small space. One side is devoted to pipe clamp storage, complete with dowels to store short pieces of pipe. The center dowel holds pipe couplers. Notice how each clamp sits in its own set of notches. This way, they always stay straight and never fall over into one another. The other side of the clamp rack holds spring and bar clamps. I built drawers near the bottom for storing extra clamp accessories. My cart can easily be kept out of the way in the shop—it rides on four casters—yet can be rolled into place whenever a bigger job demands it.

Peter VanWyk
Sheboygan Falls, Wisconsin

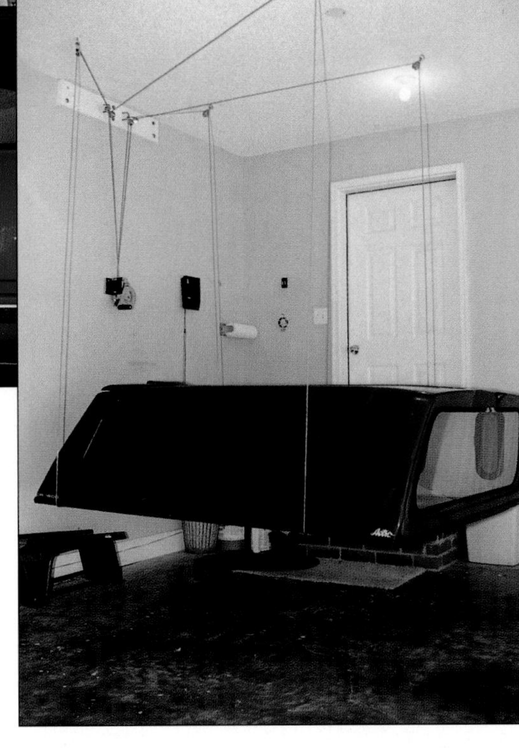

Tip-top topper storage

I prefer not to have the topper covering my pickup truck bed unless I have a specific need for it. I'm also constantly searching for more storage space in my garage. If I set the topper on the floor to store it, I'm losing valuable floor space for other things. One day I decided to develop a lift rig for my pickup topper that would create more room in my garage and get the topper out of my way.

The lift I designed provides storage for the topper when not in use and is easily operated by one person. The system employs eight pulleys, a small hand-operated boat winch, 75 to 100 ft. of coated wire cable and lag-type eyebolts. I bolted the boat winch on the garage wall in front of the truck using lag bolts and a corner bracket I fashioned myself. I hung four pulleys from the ceiling with eyebolts, positioned in a square that matches the dimensions of my topper.

Next, I attached two runs of cable to the winch. The cables thread through the pulleys and form two large loops as the photos on this page illustrate. The cables need to be long enough to loop around the bottom of the topper near the floor.

Here's how the system works: After I back the truck into the garage, I unfasten the topper from the truck bed, place a cable loop under each end of the topper and hoist the topper up to the ceiling. If you build one of these topper lifters for your garage, be sure that the truck is still able to clear the raised topper even when the cab is directly beneath it.

Besides being easy to install (it took me less than a day once I'd gotten all of the parts together), this lift frees up valuable garage floor space, keeps your topper out of harm's way and is fairly inexpensive to build.

Marlin Quarberg
Russellville, Arkansas

Stackable hardware holders save space

These accessory organizers take up no workbench space in the workshop. I made mine from scrap materials I found in my shop. Each two-compartment organizer is made from plywood with a clear plastic front panel. This way, it's easy to see the contents at a glance. To store mine, I created vertical storage racks with cleats to support each compartment. The compartments provide ample storage space for a wide range of items, but especially for various kinds of hardware. If you model yours after mine, the organizers slide in and out on the cleats like miniature drawers.

James W. Smith
Ramsen, New York

Finally, a place to retire to after retiring

The photo at right shows my workbench before I retired, which explains why I designed the shop storage system you see above. With 20 drawers and a cabinet in the workbench, I'm now able to store nearly every shop tool and supply I own. I have designated each drawer to hold something specific. All of my wood screws go in one, nuts and bolts in another, electrical supplies in another, and so forth.

All of the materials for this project came from pine trees logged off my property and sawed into boards at my brother's portable mill eight years ago. As an added decorative touch, I used dovetail joints on all the corners of the drawers. The drawers themselves measure 20 in. wide by 24 in. long and vary in depths of 4, 6 and 11 in. They are set on mechanical drawer slides that can be purchased in many sizes at most home centers and hardware stores.

Not only has this shop organization project made it easier for me to find the items that I need, but it also has freed up valuable workbench and floor space—something most handymen can never have enough of.

Calvin Cromwell
Westport, Maine

Index